Thanks

Chef
Julio Rodriguez

Thanks for your help Ann!

DJalores

Doll's Kitchen

La Cocina De Dolly

by

Julio Rodriguez

authorHOUSE®

AuthorHouse™
1663 Liberty Drive, Suite 200
Bloomington, IN 47403
www.authorhouse.com
Phone: 1-800-839-8640

First published by AuthorHouse 10/29/2007

ISBN: 978-1-4343-1413-0 (sc)

Printed in the United States of America
Bloomington, Indiana

This book is printed on acid-free paper.

Introduction

Meet Julio Rodriquez and Dolores "Dolly" Batista

This book is dedicated to Dolores (Doll) Batista, my best friend and companion for many wonderful years and to the many fantastic meals I've cooked for our many friends and social gatherings at our home. The dishes are mostly Hispanic by nature however they can easily be changed to suit various nationalities, by simply changing the spices or the base product to create a new and exciting dish.

My name is Julio Rodriguez , I was born in Aguas Buenas, Puerto Rico, when I came to New York I wanted to be a artist, little did I realize that the art that I would love most would be in the kitchen, cooking. Graduating from high school in the Bronx, I enlisted in the U.S. Navy where there was no need for an artist, which had been my major. I was then offered two choices in training, laundry or commissary, Hmm I thought, clean clothes or a full stomach, I chose the stomach. Soon thereafter I started my culinary training by attending a commissary school at the Newport Military Academy in Rhode Island for 6 months. That tour of duty turned out to be a blessing in disguise as I later found out that I could use my knowledge of all those 8 years of art and apply them to creating beautiful dishes. After my tour with the Navy I went on to various restaurants cooking my way through New York until finally, I ended up teaching Culinary Arts and, today writing my first book on the fine Art of Cuisine. I now invite you to view my art in the following pages; subsequently the study of colors becomes very important, for as you well know, food must first look good to the eye before it reaches the mouth.

This book is of much importance to the beginner because it will cover which pot or pan to use, which knife, which spice and their uses, how much fire (heat) under the pan or pot, when to boil or simmer, when to fry, sauté, how to prepare soups, stews, the use of vegetables, meats, from steaks to ground beef, poultry, fish, and shellfish, how to prepare rice and beans, pastas, omelets, salads, mushrooms, how to bake and prepare desserts. I even included a section for Italian foods. We Hispanics have a love affair with pastas, especially lasagnas. I also threw in some gourmet dishes that I hope you enjoy. I almost forgot the cute little stories on our travels and tribulations with pictures of Doll and some of our friends on our vacations and dinners at home. The names are the same we did not protect the innocent.

I finally decided to write a cookbook because of the many times I've heard my friends say "you cook so good maybe you should write a book" So here it is guys, now go out there and buy it.

The little girl on the cover is Dolores "Dolly" Batista at the age of 18 months.

Table of Contents

MIXING AND MEASURING

Measurements are important for large items, as in baking where accurate amounts are critical for correct results, for smaller items a pinch or dash will do, the amount of spice is based on the taste or visual measurement. Remember <u>do not over season</u>.

MEASURING CUP AND SPOONS.

MEASURING SPOONS: a good idea to have a set of four to measure accurately, regular spoons are not accurate enough.

MEASURING CUPS usually have measurements outlined on the outside of the cup.

MIXING AND SIEVING: wooden spoons are very helpful in the kitchen; they stand up to heat without burning your hand.

WOODEN SPATULA: Good for folding mixtures, i.e.: egg whites and chocolate.

COLANDER: Buy the self standing type with two handles for draining vegetables and Pastas.

SIEVES: Two sizes, small and large for sifting dry ingredients and draining fruit, vegetables and pastas.

LADLE: For serving hot liquids such as soups, and stews

SERVING SPOON: For serving Large Portions.

SLOTTED SPOONS: Removing food from hot water and skimming scum from the surface of liquids.

BALLON WHISK: Whisking Eggs, mixing Dressings.

BOWLS: Have various sizes, glass is best and gives you a view of what you are mixing.

BOX GRATER: Great for grating cheese, vegetables etc.

POTATO MASHER: Mash those potatoes and vegetables.

BLENDERS: Use to puree foods, soups, butter, dips.

TONGS: Must have tongs for moving hot pieces of food around.

Measuring spoons

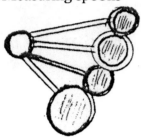

Measuring Cup

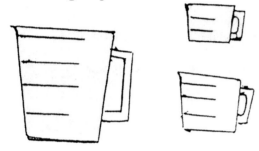

Wooden Spoon

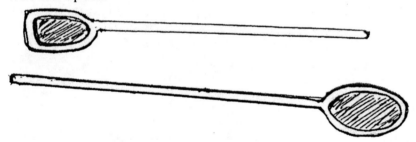

Colander

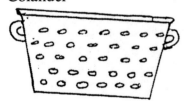

Sieves

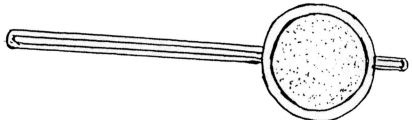

Ladle

Serving Spoon

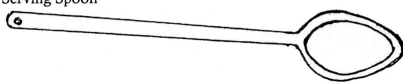

Wooden Spatula

Bowls

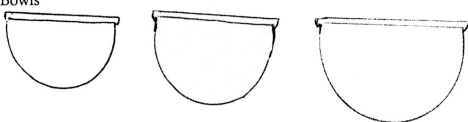

POTS AND PANS

Perhaps the most important pieces of equipment in your kitchen, therefore when it comes to buying pots and pans, buy good ones, they will last for years, with time saved and less burned food. You will need to buy two or three deep pots and at least one shallow pan for sautéing' or frying. Stainless steel is best for heat, durability and cleaning.

SAUCE PAN (small): For heating water, milk, or other small items.

SAUCE PAN (medium): Multifunctional pan for sauces, stews, vegetables, soups.

SAUCE PAN (Large): Multifunctional pan used for larger meals.

SMALL SAUTE PAN: Used for omelets, crepes, small sauté items or vegetables

MEDIUM SAUTE PAN: For use when larger quantities are required.

LARGE SAUTE PAN, OR SAUCE PAN: A good strong pan with various uses for sautéing, frying, boiling, steaming or stir frying.

LARGE SAUTE PAN OR FRYING PAN: a good strong pan with various uses from sautéing, frying, boiling, steaming or stir frying.

CALDERO: A large cast iron or aluminum kettle. For preparing large dishes, rice, soups, stews,

BAKING AND ROASTING:

These pans are not used every day so you don't need to buy the best but always try to buy quality products.

BAKING DISH: Ceramic or Stainless Steel (8" x 10") 3 to 4in deep.

For making Pasta dishes as in Lasagna, Stuffed Shells or Stuffed Roasted Peppers. Baked Chicken, Roast Duck and Baked Turkey. You'll also find many uses for Baking Desserts

STOVE TOP GRILL: Any grilled food: Hamburgers, chicken, frankfurters, and vegetables

Heating should be kept at a medium to low level when cooking.

Same rule applies to baking; 300° to 400° is the medium rule.

SMALL   MEDIUM   LARGE

SAUTE PANS/*FRYING PANS ALSO COME IN SMALL, MEDIUM, AND LARGE.*

LARGE POT OR KETTLE

STOVE TOP GRILL

CUTTING BOARDS

KNIVES

Good quality knives are important, remember you must be careful, and your knives should be sharp and kept in a wooden block.

Always make sure to curl your fingers when holding an item for cutting.

SERRATED KNIFE: 3" blade knife is used for slicing tomatoes and other vegetables.

PARING KNIFE: This is a fine knife for slicing, peeling onions, peppers, and coring apples.

CHEFS KNIFE: The most used all purpose knife with an 8" blade. Proper use is to maintain the tip of the knife on the board, moving the knife up and down while cutting, and curl those fingers!

CARVING KNIFE: This 8" flexible and thin knife carves meat in thin slices

CARVING FORK: holds the meat firmly while carving on angle, away from you.

SHARPENING STEEL: To keep knives sharp. Move the knife blade down the steel on an angle, repeat several times. Wipe knife before using.

CUTTING BOARD: (wood) clean well after use.

LARGE AND SMALL SPATULAS: Shaped like a knife, used for spreading icing on cakes, cookies, lasagna.

Serrated Knife

Paring Knife

Chef's knife

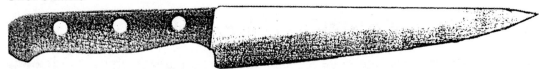

Carving Knife

Carving Fork

Sharpening Steel

Cutting Board

Large and small Spatulas

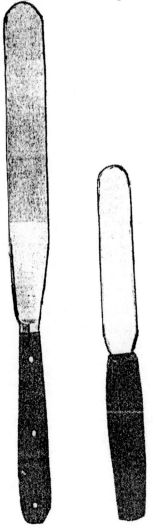

Tongs

Ballon Whisk

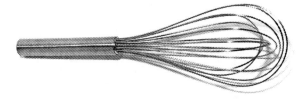

Slotted spoons

Box Grater

Potato masher

Blender

Food Processor

HEATING

How much or how little heat is **very important** in cooking, baking and roasting.

I've always said to my students if you are not sure how much heat to use, stick with medium heat, and in baking or roasting 350 degrees F is average. What you do not want is to burn food, burning will change the flavor of almost any meal you are trying to prepare.

Low heat:

Medium heat:

Medium high:

High:

When to cover or uncover a pot

Perhaps you have heard the old saying "A watched pot never boils"

Boiling is when the bubbles burst. A covered pot concentrates steam if your cover is about to blow it's because your heat is too high, also in many cases it is good to cover

70% of the top. If what you are cooking is foaming over the side of your pot, again too much heat, stir constantly, this is very important especially when making a sauce you don't want high heat. A sauce needs to simmer slowly and be stirred constantly, by doing so it prevents the sauce sticking to the bottom of the pot or pan and burning.

TERMS

Adobo: A mixture of spices: Garlic, pepper, salt, turmeric, and cumin

Aji: Scotch bonnet Pepper, (a small bonnet sized green, yellow, red rounded hot, hot, hot, pepper) use small quantities. Very good for making home made hot sauces or jerk chicken.

Ajises: Often called ajisito. A small mild to hot chili green pepper. Used for making sofrito use in beans and stews, Hispanic and mediteranean cooking.

Alcaparrado: Capers, little pungent buds from the caper plant, in a vinegar brine, used in chicken, fish, beans, soups, stews, salads etc.

Bacalao: Salted or unsalted Codfish or Haddock, fresh sliced, or fillet with or without bones

Bacalaoito: A small batter fried codfish fritter.

Bijol: A condiment used for color. Contains cumin, corn flour and yellow food coloring. Use in place of saffron.

Calabasa: Pumpkin. A large round squash firm with orange or yellow sweet flesh, great additive for soups, stews, beans, as a vegetable and in custards.

Caldero: A round cast aluminum large pot. Comes in various sizes. We keep a very large one at home for those special occasions of rice for 20 or 30 friends.

Chorizo: Smoked pork sausages, high in seasoning and paprika, Comes wrapped in plastic, or in cans. Various lengths from 2 to 6 or 8 inches. Great for rice, beans, soups, or as an appetizer.

Coco: Coconut, hard shell, fresh, with white meat and milk. Use for rice, fish, and custard as well as many tropical drinks.

Cumino: Cumin, a pungent flavorful seed, ground and used in beans, stews, Cuban, Spanish, and Mediterranean dishes.

Empanada: Fried or baked pastry type turnover, stuffed with beef, chicken, seafood, vegetables or whatever suits your taste.

Escabeche: Marinated pickled Cod fish, swordfish, shrimps, or octopus.

Habichuelas: Beans. Pinto, kidney, white, black, a Spanish staple often combined with rice, (rice & beans).

Jamon: Ham, cooking ham used mostly in Hispanic dishes such as Rice and beans, soups, and stews.

Lemon & Lime: Both lemon and lime are excellent marinades for fish, chicken and soups

Minced: Any item that is finely chopped

Mir-pois: Mir pois is a French word for a mix of vegetables that start most recipes. Your basic Mir-pois is chopped onions, peppers, celery, and tomato; it's a basic mix for soups and many other dishes, mushrooms are also added for seafood dishes.

               In Spanish dishes the celery is often left out unless it is for a soup. We basically use the onion, pepper, sweet chili peppers, and tomato with cilantro, which makes our Mir-pois which we call sofrito.

Orangesour: A bitter citrus fruit juice use for marinates. You can substitute lemon or lime juice.

Platano: Plantain, The green variety is hard and unripe, used for plantain chips or tostones, boiled it is used in soups and stews.

Maduro: Yellow Plantain, Sweet, ripe, fried, used as a side dish.

Skim: The act of removing any residue that floats to the top while cooking

Sofrito: Sautéed onions, green pepper, sweet chili pepper, garlic, cilantro, and tomato (optional). A basic spice for many Hispanic and Creole dishes.

Sherry: Dry or sweet wine, excellent for its nutlike flavor, used in many fish dishes and desserts.

Tocino: Bacon slab. If you can find it use it, adds flavor of smoked bacon

Yautia: Root vegetable, hairy skin, taste is similar to potato, but sweeter, use in soups and stews.

Yuca: Cassava, a root vegetable with starchy flesh, potato like in flavor. Used in soup or fried chips as a vegetable side dish.

SPICES, SEASONINGS, SOFRITO, HERBS

SPICES ... Are to a cook like a bag of tricks to a magician, however one must remember to use them in small amounts, because spices can make a meal delicious or they can ruin it. Spices will bring about the required flavor, so easy does it, until you learn how to fully use them.

Let's start with the most used items Salt and Pepper.

Both are almost always used in cooking and as table condiments.

Type: Table Salt, Free Flowing, Refined for table use or when cooking.

Course Salt: Medium or large-size crystals, Kosher, and Sea salt are strong in taste

Remember you can always add salt at the table, but you can't take it away.

Black Pepper; All peppers enhance or awaken flavor

Type: Whole Ground black pepper.

Peppercorns and Mixed Peppercorns are a colorful blend of whole black, green, pink, white and allspice berries.

Hot Pepper Flakes, a dried, crushed <u>hot</u> red pepper, used sparingly

Pie Spice, a ground sweet spice, contains allspice, cinnamon, mace, coriander, cloves and nutmeg. Used as a seasoning for pies.

Cloves: Sweet in flavor very aromatic, used in decorating and flavoring baked ham. Ground cloves are used for baked products and fruit desserts.

Coriander: aromatic with a taste of orange, whole or ground, used in Indian dishes, meats, poultry, and in vegetables.

Cumin: very distinctive in flavor, used in Cuban, Mexican, Puerto Rican and Indian dishes, great in beans especially black beans.

Saffron: pungent, aromatic, bitter, very expensive spice, therefore use small amounts: Used in food color (yellow) rice and seafood dishes (paella).

Turmeric: a musky flavor, used to color rice, Indian curries, and bean dishes.

Cinnamon: spicy sweet in flavor, fruits, pies, cakes, cookies, custards, ground or in sticks.

Nutmeg: Sweet and pungent in flavor, ground or grated fresh when needed.

Use nutmeg in sweet dishes and desserts (Egg Nog).

Paprika: mild or hot pepper used in many Spanish dishes also as a color garnish.

Cayenne: hot chili flavor, used in Mexican and Cuban dishes.

Chili Powder: Blends of chilis, garlic, cumin, and oregano used in Mexican, Indian and Southwestern dishes.

Curry Powder: A spice mixture some are sweet others are hot. Used in Indian, Thai and Jamaican dishes, Chicken, Pork, Fish, and Rice Dishes.

ANNOTO (ACHIOTE)

A tropical seed, cooked in oil, then strained, the oil is used for coloring Arroz con Pollo, (Rice with Chicken) and Pasteles. In these days "Bihol," a powdered form of Achiote is widely used.

DRY HERBS

Basil: Flavor is sweet, spicy, minty, and great for long cooking sauces and casseroles.

Bay Leaves: Flavor is Pungent best when leaves are fresh, used in Stocks, sauces, stews, beans and seafood.

Coriander: Seed, confections, leaves for salads, great in oriental and Middle Eastern food.

Dill: Flavor subtle anise, use in marinades and dressing, great with salmon and vegetables especially cucumbers.

Oregano: Flavors most sauces, stews and pasta dishes.

Parsley: Bring out the flavor, decorative, high in vitamin C.

Sage: Flavor is bitter, used in turkey, pork, duck, chicken, veal, sausages and stuffing's.

Sofrito: A mixture of various ingredients, cilantro, garlic, onion, green pepper, oregano, and oil blended.

Rosemary: Flavor is pungent and spicy but refreshing to taste and smells great as a marinade for lamb, veal, pork and chicken or Italian cooking.

Thyme: Aromatic foliage seasoning, soups, stews, chicken, rice.

I love hot sauce, (OK I don't love, nobody really loves hot sauce but we say so. Hispanic's have a love affair with hot sauce because we make it at home and it's there on the kitchen table waiting like a secret friend. Hot sauce has found its way in many homes throughout America especially in the southwest. its popularity exist all over the world, people love to add that extra kick at the end to a steak, fish, or a chicken dish. My favorite is with soups or stews and when I eat raw clams. I once made a hot sauce that I called Dragons Fire and you can tell by its name that this sauce was hot, hot, hot. I would tell whoever wanted some to use only a 1/4 teaspoon and to sneak up on it and never ever put your nose directly in the jars opening, for the rush of heat brought tears to many eyes.

Then there was the time I was teaching a class on Culinary Arts. We were making hot sauce and I had just opened four jalapeno peppers. I was taking out the seeds by hand when nature called, I rinsed my hands in the kitchen sink dried them and headed for the bathroom. Upon finishing I once again washed and dried my hands and returned to the classroom, no sooner had I continued the lesson that a warm feeling started and quickly rose in temperature in my pants. The essence of the jalapeno seeds had entered my skin and passed on to whatever I touched. My students got a good laugh that day as I ran out the classroom for a birdbath in the middle of the day. So a good lesson to remember is to use a knife to remove the seeds and never put your hands on your eyes or any other parts of your body unless you scrub well and use plenty of soap. The seeds in many hot peppers contain the heat that makes the sauce hot. I have outlined the sweet and hot peppers for you, and remember that you are using hot pepper sauce in your cooking, easy does it, you can always add more at the end, don 't ruin your meal, if you play with fire you might get burned.

Habanero: name means from Havana, The legendary 10-alarm pepper from the Caribbean, long ago migrated to Central America where they remain very popular today. A close relative to the Scotch Bonnets from Haiti and Jamaica, the short orange pepper has a delicious, pungent, smoky quality unlike any other pepper and has a flavor and aroma that's excellent in sauces and salsas.

Aji:(red) 3 to 5 inch orange and red peppers good for home made sauce or dried into powder for sauces and stews.

Aji: Dulce Looks like the Habanero. green, orange and red colors This variety is very popular with Latinos for sofritos, it offers the same flavor and aroma of the Habanero with only a hint of heat.

Anaheim: The new Mexican chili, pungent fruity and deep green in color, smooth 7 inches long, excellent for canning, found in many Mexican stores.

Ancho: Mildly hot, fresh when green and stuffed into chili rellenos. They mature into dark rust red, they are rich in flavor and ground into powder.

Big Chili: 5 to 10 inches long, used in roasting, very mild, popular in Italian and Mexican dishes or as an appertizer.

Bolivian Rainbow: A beautiful pepper, a rainbow of colors small cone shaped, very hot edible peppers.

Bulgarian Carrot: bright orange peppers with shape and color of carrots, but quite hot, yet fruity, great in chutneys, sauces, and salsas.

Cascabella: A favorite for pickling, this pepper is yellow but will turn red, another variety is the Cascabel, which is more pungent and globe-shaped.

Charleston Hot: no it's not a dance, A hot cayenne 4 inch long pepper yellow, orange and red when ripe. Good for sauces and salsas mix.

Chile de Arbol: A cayenne type pepper, very popular in Mexico, ground into powder when dried for red chile sauces and added to soups and stews.

Cherry Bomb Hybrid: Pungent round and oval, medium hot.

Caribbean Red: A habanero variety found in the Caribbean, fiercely hot pepper. This is the one you must be very careful with, wonderful for salsas, marinades, and making your own hot sauce.

Making Hot Sauce at home

Making hot sauce at home is easy, just save one of those empty jars that we throw away, for instance, pickle, olives, spaghetti sauce, apple sauce or any other glass container with the lid. Wash the glass container well, next and most important is the type of hot peppers you want to use. Grow your own if you so desire. "Grow my own" Yes, grow your own. Come on guys, this really is a simple process. (I) Buy some hot pepper seeds, at Home Depot or any hardware store that sells soil during springtime. Some came already potted and growing Water once a week with water that has been left out at room temperature (never over water) the roots of the plant should seek out the water. Grow the peppers until they are red, then pick and put them into the glass container half full. Yes you can mix and match with various types of peppers. Add two or three crushed garlic cloves, (1) bay leaf and continue by filling the remainder with equal parts of water, vinegar, and olive oil. Cover and refrigerate. The breakdown of the peppers within a month will give you hot sauce. You can use the sauce and add more peppers and the liquid as you go along and your sauce will continue to produce or you can blend the contains at any time and have quick hot sauce. My dragons fire hot sauce was with me for 7 years. I just kept adding to it as I used it.

Empty Jar
Mixed Peppers, half full
Bay leaf
3 Garlic cloves
Olive oil
Vinegar
Water

If you wish you can add salt and black pepper to taste, others will add fresh basil, oregano or a cilantro leaf for show and flavor. Good Luck.

SANITATION

Sanitation is very important in food preparation especially in large restaurants and in catering establishments, start out with a clean kitchen and continue cleaning as you go along, this way you don 't have as much to clean up when you're finished. First your sink should be free of dishes; you'll need that space for cleaning meats, poultry, seafood, and whatever it is that becomes dirty during cooking. The cutting board is one item that needs constant cleaning especially when you finish cutting a chicken and then a green pepper or onion is required, in this case a second board would be nice but most homes don 't keep two cutting hoards. The cutting board should be made of wood and should be large enough to hold a cut up chicken. 12x12 is a good size. Never cut different meats for example chicken and then steak, there is always a danger of cross contamination. Cross contamination occurs when raw meats or eggs come in contact with foods that will be eaten uncooked This is a major source of food poisoning. Use raw meats within or 2 days of purchase, or freeze for longer storage. Contamination can also happen in the refrigerator where a steak leaks blood into another food source. This can be avoided by using proper containers for storage, especially when foods are being defrosted It is critical to cook to a safe internal temperature to avoid e-coli and to destroy bacteria that is present.

Personal hygiene is important, so if you sneeze into your hands, quickly wash using detergent and let us not forget that bathroom visit, always wash up after every visit. Food that falls on the floor in most cases should be discarded or rinsed. Mayonnaise is another product that should be kept under controlled temperature, so make sure that the macaroni and potato salads are placed in a container with ice or kept refrigerated between servings especially during those hot summer days.

Seafood is another item that spoils easily, Again all that is required is maintaining the temperature low. How often do we take a steak or chicken out of the freezer in the morning and leave it out all day as you go off to work expecting to came home to find our meat defrosted. The next time simply leave it in the refrigerator or marinate it overnight. Remember if it doesn't look or smell right, throw it out, don't take the chance, Salmonella poisoning is no joke. Mold is another item that is too familiar in the refrigerator. This happens when you open a can or jar and you use a spoon to scoop out a portion of it's contents with the spoon that you were using to mix the beans, well you just cross contaminated whatever was in that jar or can and in a few days you will have mold. Air tight containers became infected easily, so make sure that you use a clean spoon when removing part of the contents. Storage of food products in large establishments require good strong containers because of roaches, mice and rats

The USDA has four simple words to remind us of these rules:

COOK, SEPARATE, CLEAN, CHILL

MY MOTHER DOESN'T MAKE IT LIKE THAT

My mother doesn't make it like that. That was the remark I used to hear when I was teaching culinary Arts at The Henry Street Settlement in New York years ago. Yes that's not the way mom makes it at home because cooking at home is done with all the time and care in the world. However cooking in a restaurant is slightly different in a restaurant the kitchen personnel shows up four to five hours before the doors open to the public and we do preparation for every thing from salads, soups, vegetables, gravies, desserts, specials of the day, plus preparations for private parties, weddings, general catering services and the list goes on and on. Mother takes her sweet time and add lots of love to what she's cooking and they have you in mind "this is the way my baby likes it" We chefs have no idea who we're cooking for, But we know that when those doors open, and one hundred hungry people fill up the room, they want to eat in 1/2: hour or less. So if you ever wondered how' is it possible that they can feed 100 so quickly its because we have been here all day or we started the day before. I personally would like nothing more than to have a sweet chunky mom in the kitchen give me a big hug and a kiss and tell me to go watch television while she prepares a wonderful meal; but mom is gone and Gaspar the chef at Rino's Restaurant where I eat on occasions doesn't always shave.

MARINADE

Marinades are easy to mix and they add great flavor to chicken, beef, pork, and seafood.

You can mix your own by simply adding together garlic, chopped fresh herbs, olive oil, plus salt and pepper.

The herbs are: oregano, rosemary, sage, parsley, coriander, bay leaves, dill leaves, marjoram, and thyme.

A marinade can contain dry spices as well, for example: paprika, black peppercorns, cloves, hot pepper flakes, and cayenne to name a few.

Vinegar, wine, lemon or limes are excellent marinades, each contains an acid or alcohol that reduces the amount of time the meat should be marinated.

Most marinades work fine within 2 to 4 hours.

Combine the meat and marinade in a sealed container or plastic bag. Do not use aluminum or cast iron, avoid using metal if possible.

There are many salad dressings and other items in your shelves or refrigerator that make perfect marinades, for example; Italian, french dressings ,soy sauce ,cidars, worstershire, teriyaki and duck sauce. Next time you order Chinese, save the little packets of soy and duck sauce for marinading and bar b ques.

TAPAS/APPETIZERS

Doll and I love tapas, or "appies" as I like to call them, at times we will be at a bar with a group of friends having drinks and we'll order appetizers from the menu, shrimps, clams, chorizos, olives, and a salad and " I'll just pick" is in style as we pass around the various tapas.

Dolores and I spent some time last year vacationing in Puerto Rico. We stayed at the Hyatt Hotel and Casino, a beautiful location by the shore, with a tapas bar that served mixed olives in a large martini glass. That visit became a regular stop on the way to the Casino, for olives and a drink.

Marinated olives satisfy two basic food cravings: salt & sour.

Following recipe serves from 8 to 10

1 Lb can or jar of unpitted large green olives
1 can of black olives unpitted
24 Picholine olives, unpitted
1 Tablespoon hot sauce (optimal)
4 Garlic cloves peeled and slightly crushed
1 lemon cut in small pieces (1/2 wedges)
4 sprigs of fresh thyme
Extra virgin olive oil to cover
Black pepper to taste
To marinate the olive, press to crack or cut the olive in half.

Put the olives, garlic, lemon wedges, thyme, black pepper and olive oil into a bowl and stir, then put the olives with the oil in a container or glass jar, seal and allow to stand at room temperature for 24 hours, then refrigerate before serving. When you are ready to serve remove the olives from the oil.

OLIVES

There are many types of olives, outlined below are some of the most popular.

Pitted Kalamata: One of the more popular black olives commonly found on Greek salads. They have a pronounced, powerful olive flavor and a high salt content. And since there are no pits you can eat them like candy.

Gaeta: Plump, dark purple Italian olives with very tender, almost melt-away, texture, on the sour side.

Provencal: A medium-green French olive, marinated in a mix of basil, fragrant lavender, thyme, fennel, savory, and rosemary. The herbs hit you in the nose first, followed by the olive and salt flavors. A really interesting balance of herbal aroma and olive taste.

Picholine: A slender, full flavored green olive from the south of France. Sweet (as olives go) with a nice, crunchy texture.

Black Alfonsos: Soft skinned Chilean olive with very tender flesh. Similar in texture to a small plum. They are cured in wine vinegar for a satisfying sour/salt rush.

Phoenica House Blend: Lebanese green olives marinated in herbs and packed in olive oil. Heavy on the garlic.

Green Greek cracked: Crunch flesh flavored with lemon and stored in vinegar. Good bowl or antipasto olive.

Moroccan oil-cured: These black olives have a wrinkled, leathery surface from the dry salt curing process. Since they retain more of their natural bitterness they can be eaten straight.

Spicy: Cracked green olives in a powerful chili pepper/vinegar marinade the consistency of tomato sauce. The after burn sits on your tongue for a spell and hurts real good.

Jalapeño Stuffed: Huge, crisp green California olives cured Sicilian-style and stuffed with pickled jalapeño. Both flavors remain distinct and complement each other nicely without either dominating. A great alternative martini olive or accompaniment for tequila.

Garlic Stuffed: Always save the best for last. Another good martini olive, it's the same California Colossal olive stuffed with a pickled garlic clove. If you like garlic, you'll want to inhale a pound in a single sitting.

ALCAPURRIAS

½ pound of ground pork meat or beef 1/2 salt pork
1 ounce cooking ham
2 tablespoons of sofrito
½ teaspoon of dried oregano
½ teaspoon of olive oil
½ teaspoon of Bijol (food coloring)
½ teaspoon of salt
¼ teaspoon of black pepper
4 large pimento stuffed olives (chopped)
½ teaspoon of capers
5 very green bananas
2 pounds of yucca (taro root)
2 teaspoons of salt
½ teaspoon Bijol
1 tablespoon of melted cooled shortening

Fill a bowl with salted water. Peel the bananas and taro root and as you peel place them into the salt water. If you are going to use a grater use the fine side and grate the vegetables into a plastic bowl. Note: If you have a food processor cut the vegetables into small pieces and process until fine. Add the salt, Bijol and shortening and mix well. Refrigerate for 3 hours or for best results overnight.

In a frying pan brown the meat. Once browned add all the remaining ingredients and stir well than cook at medium heat for 15 minutes. Taste the meat for seasoning; add more salt if needed to taste.

Heat 2 cups of vegetable oil to 375 degrees. Take a large piece of aluminum paper and place a little oil on top and smear it around. Spread about 1/4 cup of the alcapurria dough onto the aluminum paper. Place a tablespoon of the meat filling in the middle and flip one side of the dough over using the aluminum paper to cover the meat with the dough (masa) until the dough is complete as one oblong shape. Using a spoon help glide the dough gently into the hot oil. Cook until golden brown on both sides, Turn over once and using a slotted spoon carefully take out the alcapurrias and put them on paper towels (both sides) to remove some of the oil.

COD FISH FRITTERS
BACALAITOS

¼ lb. bacalao filet
¾ cup flour
½ tsp. baking powder
1/3 tsp salt
1/3 tsp oregano
¾ cup bacalao broth
1 tsp. black pepper
2 tsp. crushed garlic
oil for frying

Purchase the processed bacalao that is not dry and does not need to be soaked for a long time, get the deboned bacalao

Rinse the bacalao and tear into small pieces. Boil in plenty of water for about 20 minutes. Discard water and add fresh water and, boil again for another 20 minutes. Let it cool in the water and then save the water. Remove the bacalao and drain in a metal drainer and wait for it to cool down. Once cool to the touch, tear the fish into smaller pieces and set it aside. .

In a medium bowl combine the flour, baking powder, salt, pepper, and garlic, add the broth and whisk. The mixture should look like pancake batter. Then add the drained bacalao and whisk again. If the batter seems too thick just add a little more of the bacalao broth and whisk. If you put too much broth add a little bit of flour.

Spoon the batter by ½ cup (1/2 cup will make one bacalaito) the bacalaitos should be fried over medium-high heat turning only once. They should be a golden color on both sides. Drain on paper towels before serving.

Any extra fish or batter may be frozen for later use.

The above listed amounts will give you 10 bacalaitos.

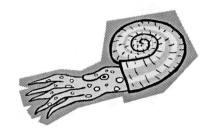

CALAMARES/SQUID

1 Lb squid
All purpose flour coating
1 cup vegetable or corn oil for deep frying
1 lemon cut into wedges

The squid you buy in the fish store requires cleaning, start with removing the head and then take out the clear backbone and rinse the calamare tube.

Slice the squid into 1 inch rings, rinse and dry well on paper towels, Do not season the squid or the flour, lightly coat the squid in flour, don't forget the heads, heat the oil in a deep frying pan at medium high heat. Carefully add the squid and fry until golden brown 2 to 3 minutes. Do not over cook, the squid will become tough and rubbery instead of moist and tender, if overcooked. Using a slotted spoon remove the squid from the oil and allow to drain on paper towels, sprinkle with salt and pepper. Serve with salsa , tartar sauce, or cocktail sauce, and lemon wedges.

Serves 6

SHRIMPS IN LEMON OR LIME SAUCE
CAMARONES EN SALSA DE LEMON

12 jumbo shrimps with shells
4 tablespoons olive oil
3 lemon or limes
2 garlic cloves, finely chopped
splash of dry sherry or white wine
salt & pepper to taste
parsley or cilantro for garnish

To prepare the shimps leave the shell and tail intact

Use a sharp knife and cut along the back and devein each shrimp. Rinse the shrimp under cold water and dry on a paper towel. Heat the olive oil in a large skillet pan then add the garlic and the shrimp, cook for 5 minutes, stirring constantly, mix in the juice of 2 lemons or limes, a splash of dry wine or sherry. Grate one lemon or lime and add the lemon/lime zest to the shrimps. Transfer the shrimps to a serving dish, season to taste with salt & pepper and garnish with parsley or cilantro chopped fine. Serve with lemon or lime wedges.

CHICKEN LIVERS IN SHERRY SAUCE WITH ONIONS
HIGADO DE POLLO EN VINO CON CEBOLLA

1 lb chicken livers
3 tablespoons olive oil
2 garlic cloves, crushed
1 onion sliced
½ cup dry sherry or white dry wine
salt and pepper to taste
½ teaspoon oregano
½ teaspoon adobo seasoning
1 sprig of cilantro

Heat a frying pan and add the olive oil, garlic and onions, sauté the onions until soft, about 5 minutes, add the chicken livers and continue cooking for 5 minutes, now add the salt, pepper, and the wine, cover and simmer for 5 more minutes, garnish with cilantro and serve.

This dish is a great "Tapas appetizer" or it can be the entrée with white rice.

Making the dough:

3 cups of unbleached all purpose flour
4 tablespoons of chilled butter (lard is a good substitute)
1 ½ teaspoon salt
1 ¼ cups (10 ounces) cold water

In a large mixing bowl combine the flour and chilled butter until the mix resembles cornmeal, add the salt to the water, stir well then, add water to the flour-butter mix. Mix gently with a fork until you get a rough dough, if you have to add more water do so one tablespoon at a time until the dough holds together. Put the dough onto a lightly floured board and knead with your palm until smooth, 2 to 3 minutes, wrap it in plastic wrap and refrigerate for 30 minutes.

Remove the dough from the refrigerator and put in on a lightly floured surface, cut into 4 pieces, roll out each piece with a rolling pin until you have the thickness you desire, then cut each piece using a can or jar as a cuter to obtain a circular pattie dough shape. Patties can be filled with almost anything you can think of, beef is still # 1, chicken, seafood, cheese and vegetables are also popular.

Simply stew the item you wish to fill the dough with, then cool, put the product or filler in one part of the dough, now add water with your fingers around the edge of the circular dough, this process will help to keep the ends from opening, with a fork lightly punch 2 to 3 holes on top of dough, use a fork to press on edges, this procedure tightens the ends and decorates the pattie. Fry in medium hot oil until golden brown or bake at 350 degrees F until golden brown, 20 to 30 minutes.

*If you do not wish to go through all this work of mixing the dough, simply go to your local supermarket or grocer and obtain the pattie dough which comes in a package of a dozen.

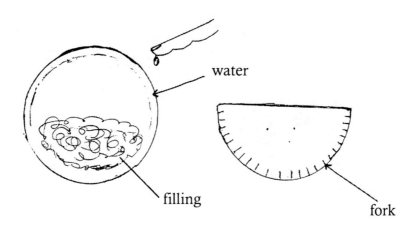

water

filling

fork

STEWING CHICKEN OR BEEF FOR PATTIES

First decide how many patties you wish to make, this recipe is for 10 patties.

Chicken: 1 breast cut into small pieces.
    Or
Beef: 1 lb ground beef

½ red pepper, diced
½ green pepper diced
½ onion, diced
1 sprig of cilantro
6 pimento stuffed olives, chopped
1 tablespoon sofrito (optional)
½ small can of tomato sauce
½ teaspoon of oregano
2 tablespoons olive oil

Heat a sauce pan to medium heat, then add olive oil add the beef or chicken meat, cook uncovered stirring frequently for 5 minutes, now add the peppers, garlic, onion, salt and pepper and stir while cooking for another 5 minutes, finally add the remaining ingredients and cook covered for 10 more minutes, at this time the stewing is complete. Allow the meat to cool before putting into the Pattie dough.

* For vegetable Pattie, omit chicken or beef; add your favorite vegetable, zucchini, mushroom, tomato, potato, cabbage or whatever you wish.

* For seafood Pattie, add seafood to the mix and stew away.

Just remember the filling should not be too saucy or juicy, but somewhat dry.

CHORIZOS (SPANISH SAUSAGE)

Chorizos come in many varieties and sizes, some are thick, others thin, plain or smoked, some are canned others are bagged. I could cook almost every dish that I make, with chorizo, that's how much I like chorizo, they are easy to prepare and add a lot of flavor to eggs, soups, stews, rice dishes or as an appetizer with bread.

Chorizos are cured using smoked Spanish paprika; it gives meats a deep red color and rich smoky flavor.

Salchichones are cured with black pepper instead of paprika, and Morcillas are a blood sausage cured with onion or rice, great for stews and grilling. So here's a quick recipe.

Chorizo, garlic, peppers and red wine.

2 Chorizo cut 1 ½ to 2 inch slices
½ Green pepper cut in small squares
½ Red pepper cut in small squares
½ Onion, chopped
2 Garlic cloves, crushed
4 tablespoons olive oil
½ Cup of dry red wine
Salt and pepper to taste
2 Tablespoons parsley, chopped fine

Heat a skillet or frying pan add olive oil and garlic, pepper and onion, stir for 3 minutes set aside, using the same pan, add the chorizo and sauté stirring constantly for about 5 minutes, add the pepper and onion mix, put in the wine, cook for 2 minutes, add salt and pepper to taste and parsley. Serve as an appetizer or side dish.

We use wine when we cook, sometimes it ends up in the food

CREOLE GARLIC SAUCE
MOJO CRIOLLO

Mojo criollo is not for the faint hearted, it is a truly potent garlic sauce. Most of the variations served at American and Spanish restaurants are only imitations. Mojo is served with yucca, most pork and chicken dishes, and with root vegetables and olive oil. This sauce should be made in advance.

6 to 8 cloves of garlic
1 teaspoon salt
¼ cup each fresh lime and lemon juice
½ cup of pure Spanish olive oil
1 medium size onion, minced.

Using a mortar and pestle or a food processor, crush the garlic with the salt to form a thick paste.

In a mixing bowl, combine the garlic paste, onion, and juices; let the mixture sit at room temperature for about 30 minutes.

Minutes before you are ready to serve the mojo, heat the oil over medium high heat in a medium size pan, until it is very hot, add the garlic mixture, stir, and serve immediately. To reheat, simmer over low heat. The sauce keeps several weeks refrigerated.

Makes one cup.

YUCCA WITH GARLIC SAUCE
(YUCCA CON MOJO)

4 Medium size yuccas peeled and cut in half
The yucca can be fresh or frozen
1 large red Spanish onion sliced and lightly sautéed.
1 oz. mojo criollo
2 tablespoons finely chopped fresh parsley, optional

Fill a large saucepan to ¾ capacity, boil water and then add salt and yucca, cover and cook until tender.

Transfer the yucca to a serving bowl or platter, garnish with sliced sautéed red onion, toss with the garlic sauce and sprinkle with parsley, serve immediately.

Usually served as a side dish for Pernil (pork shoulder) and at times for breakfast.

Serves three to four

My favorite tree the Palm and there's Dolores (Doll) soaking
up the sun at Hyatt Dorado in sunny Puerto Rico

EGGPLANT, ONIONS AND BELL PEPPER DIP

1 Medium eggplant remove skin, cut into diced pieces,
1 Large green pepper, chopped
1 Large red pepper, chopped
1 Large onion, chopped
¼ Cup olive oil
2 Garlic cloves, crushed fine
The juice of one lemon or lime
2 Tablespoons chopped cilantro
½ teaspoon paprika
Salt and pepper to taste

Heat a skillet or frying pan at medium heat and add the oil, eggplant, peppers, onions, garlic, stir constantly for 20 minutes while cooking, now add the paprika, salt and pepper and lemon or lime juice, continue cooking uncovered at low heat until all items are tender and spreadable. Bake sliced Italian or French bread to a golden brown and let the party begin, don't forget the Wine.

*The eggplant can also be prepared in the oven. Cut the eggplant in half, skin on and bake at 350. f, for 30 minutes, prepare the other items in the frying pan and mix in the eggplant minus skin at the end.

ROASTED PEPPER SALAD

2 Red peppers
2 Green peppers
2 Yellow peppers
½ cup olive oil
3 Tablespoons white vinegar or lemon juice
Salt and pepper to taste
3 Garlic cloves, crushed
1 Tablespoon of capers
1 Teaspoon oregano

Put the peppers on a stove top burner and roast until the skin is blackened turning them frequently. Remove the peppers from the heat, put them on a tray and cover them with a damp towel. This measure will allow them to steam, making the removal of the skin easier. Let the peppers cool for 15 minutes, carefully cut the peppers on the side and take out the seeds, stem and core, place the peppers down and remove the burned skin with a butter knife, then cut each pepper into strips, place them in a serving dish, add the capers, olive oil, vinegar, crushed garlic and oregano.

*Garnish with black olives, cilantro or parsley.

I love clams in just about any way they are served, raw, baked, stewed, in soups, mixed, or steamed. If you put up a dozen clams, I'm sitting down to enjoying the "Frutta de mare" (fruit of the sea).

There are four major categories of Atlantic clams: hard shell, soft shell, surf clams, and razor clams. Hard large clams are also called Qua-hogs. The smallest is the little neck, they are also the most tender and besides being the most expensive they are the sweetest tasting, and are excellent raw. Medium que-hogs are also called cherry stones. Cherry stones can be eaten raw or cooked in various ways. They are perfect for stuffing. Large qua-hogs are called chowder clams, great for soups, and they are relatively inexpensive. When buying clams make sure that the shells are firmly closed.

Spanish baked clams / Almejas al horno

Like many Spanish dishes, we need a sofrito of onions, tomatoes, and garlic; I would also add mix green and red peppers for color.

24 Little neck or cherry stone clams
1 cup of dry sherry or white wine
3 to 4 chorizos chopped fine
5 Garlic cloves crushed fine
1 medium onion, finely chopped
1/3 cup extra virgin olive oil
2 medium tomatoes, finely chopped
2 peppers 1 green and 1 red, finely chopped
2 tablespoons of parsley
Salt & black pepper to taste
Juice of one lemon

First rinse the clams ,

You'll need a large pot that will hold 24 clams, apply medium heat , Steam the clams covered in the sherry or white wine for 10 to 15 minutes, or until they open, put aside and save the liquid (minus sand). In a wide sauté frying pan over medium heat, cook the garlic, onion, peppers and chorizo in the olive oil for about 10 minutes, add the clam liquid, tomatoes, stir in the parsley, salt, pepper and lemon juice. Pre heat oven to 350 degrees F., slide a knife under each clam to loosen, arrange on a baking pan, spoon the stuffing over each clam, bake the clams for 10 to 15 minutes, serve immediately.

- For clams casino: add bacon strips instead of chorizo
- Butter can be added to the stuffing, using less olive oil
- Cheese can also be added to the top of the stuffing.
  The type of cheese is up to you.

Garlic

Garlic has to be the most wonderful herb of all times, I remember shopping at a fruit and vegetable store years ago and seeing an oriental lady behind the counter eating raw garlic. She was popping down the garlic like they were grapes. Upon asking why, she explained that garlic was good for her stomach cramps. Good thing there are garlic pills available over the counter today. In doing research for Doll's Kitchen, I found out that garlic is also a cancer-cure agent and I thought Dracula had trouble with garlic. If garlic had been created in a laboratory, it would be a high priced prescription drug, because it can lower cholesterol, prevent blood clots, reduce blood pressure, prevent cancer, and protect against bacterial and fungal infections. A large number of consumers purchase garlic from health food stores and pharmacies to help bolster their immune system and cardiovascular disease, as well as a supplement for diets "Hey I thought this was a cook book" O.K. Garlic is also one of the most popular condiments used for cooking, it is great in soups, stews, chicken, meats, and sauces. The aroma of garlic and onions frying in olive oil is irresistible. Restaurants today bake the entire garlic clove with butter and serve it mixed in various dishes like garlic mashed potatoes, or a garlic spread and at times as a sauce for vegetables. Garlic is inexpensive and available just about everywhere. So go out and buy some but if you are going to eat it raw don't forget the mouthwash.

SALADS/ENSALADAS

BEAN SALADS

Bean salads are simple yet wonderful and a refreshing addition to any summer meal, picnic, or bar b que, You will find many advertised recipes for your favorite bean salad in various magazines throughout the summer, But fear not, for making a bean salad is as easy as 1, 2, 3, Lets start out by opening several cans of different types of beans. Example: black white, red beans and a can of chickpeas. The amount of beans depends largely on how many people you are going to feed. Now mince an onion, 2 garlic cloves, cilantro, add salt, pepper, oregano, and enough olive oil to coat the beans, about ¼ cup, a tablespoon of vinegar or lemon, lime juice, and presto you have bean salad, simple, right, O.K lets say you have a tomato; or various colored peppers, cube them and toss them in. The peppers can be raw or roasted (its up to you). What about chickpeas with cubed cucumbers, chopped dill, and Italian dressing? Good one, How about pigeon peas (gandules) with fried onions, olive oil and red roasted peppers ? yummy, now your getting it.

There are no set rules when it comes to salads, what you do with what you have is ok. Just make sure that it looks and taste good. Create and develop your own recipes. What about butter beans with fried chorizo or salami wedges? (yes) . Mmm I'm starting to like this. What about mixing corn and beans, (yes) a Mexican touch, don't forget the jalapenos, and red peppers. Maybe a salad made from various lentil beans (yes,). Lentils come in many colors and would make a great salad What about lima beans? (yes) lima beans are very cool, Hey I have one, what about a fresh string bean salad? Yes, a fresh string bean salad will work just fine, mix various fresh beans and after boiling, removed the water, and add olive oil and your favorite seasonings. You can create a salad with crunch by adding celery or you might want to do nuts or mix in fruits, fresh or dried So enjoy creating a bean salad and your friends will say (This salad is fantastic how did you make it) and you can smile and say, "It 's my recipe"

Remember to serve your salads cold.

1 iceberg lettuce
2oz. blue cheese
½ cup sour cream
½ cup mayonnaise
¼ cup lime juice
1 scallion minced
salt and pepper to taste
1 garlic clove smashed
2 tablespoon of olive oil
2 chorizos minced and fried
1 tablespoon of parsley

Cut a chilled iceberg lettuce in four quarters, set aside in a plastic bowl blend the blue cheese, sour cream, mayonnaise, garlic, and lime juice. After blending add the scallion and parsley, set aside.

Heat a frying pan at medium heat and add the olive oil followed by the chorizo and fry for about 3 minutes, stirring often until golden brown, allow the chorizo to cool. Plate ¼ of the lettuce and spoon over with the cream mix add 2 tablespoons of the chorizo with the olive oil on the lower part of the lettuce and plate.

Romaine, Arugula, Tomatoes and Spanish Onions Vinaigrette

½ Romaine lettuce chopped into large pieces
12 leaves of arugula remove stem and rinse well
1 large tomato diced large
I large Spanish red onion sliced
¼ cup pine nuts
½ cup Spanish olive oil
½ cup balsamic vinegar
1 teaspoon sugar
salt and pepper to taste

In a plastic bowl blend the balsamic vinegar, olive oil with salt and pepper and sugar.

In another bowl mix the romaine lettuce, arugula, red onion and pine nuts.

Just before serving mix the dressing into the salad and plate.

Serves 6

Asparagus with goat cheese and chorizo

2 pounds of medium asparagus
4 ounces of goat cheese crumbled
2 chorizo cut into thin slices
½ cup of Spanish olive oil
½ cup sherry vinegar
salt and pepper to taste

Pour about ½ inch of water into a large pot with a steamer basket and bring to a boil Cut and discard the tough end of the asparagus and add the spears to the steamer basket Cover the pot and boil for 4 to 5 minutes. Transfer the spears to paper towels and pat dry and allow to cool at room temperature. Cut each spear diagonally into two pieces each. Warm a frying pan at medium heat and add the olive oil and the chorizo slices, fry for 3 minutes, stirring constantly until golden brown. Set aside.

In a bowl blend the olive oil and the sherry vinegar with the salt and pepper add the asparagus and toss, than add the goat cheese chorizo and toss again, transfer to plates and serve.

Watercress, Spinach and Radish salad with sweet citrus mustard vinaigrette

One bunch of watercress
1/2 pound of spinach
2 radishes sliced thin
2 tablespoon orange juice
2 tablespoon grapefruit juice
1 teaspoon spicy grain mustard
2 tablespoon of Spanish olive oil
2 tablespoon balsamic vinegar
1 teaspoon sugar
salt and pepper to taste

Rinse the spinach well cut into mid size pieces and add them to a bowl with the watercress.

In a separate bowl blend the orange juice, grapefruit juice, mustard, olive oil, vinegar and sugar, and refrigerate until use.

When you are ready to serve, lightly toss the citrus mix with the spinach, watercress and serve garnish with the thin sliced radishes.

Dolores (Dolly) Favorite

Watercress with Olive oil, a touch of vinegar and a dash of salt and pepper

Spinach with Strawberries and Italian Dressing

I know this combination sounds a bit strange but try it and you 're going to love it. First take fresh spinach and rise well in a bowl; Spinach has a lot of sandy areas and there 's nothing worst than a mouthful of salad with gritty sand, so rinse, rinse, and rinse again. Next combine ½ a cup of frozen strawberries with syrup and ½ a cup of Italian dressing. The combination of the sweetness of the strawberry syrup and the sour of the Italian dressing is really good over spinach.

Tear the spinach into smaller pieces in a bowl and pour the Italian and strawberry blend over it, toss gently and serve

Avocado Salad
Ensalada de Agaucate

This is the most popular Latin salad of all, and it is served with almost any Spanish dish you can imagine and you can order it in most Spanish restaurants.

Watercress or lettuce leaves for lining the platter, (optional)
2 large ripe avocados or 4 smaller avocados, peeled, pitted, halved lengthwise and thinly sliced
1 small red Spanish onion, cut in half and the halves thinly sliced
Salt and freshly ground black pepper to taste
¼ cup pure Spanish olive oil
3 Tablespoons white vinegar or fresh lemon juice
1 teaspoon finely chopped fresh parsley

On a large platter lined with greens, arrange the avocado slices, place the onions on top, and sprinkle with salt and pepper. Whisk together the oil and vinegar and drizzle over the salad. Sprinkle with the parsley and serve.

Makes 6 Servings

We met this fruit and vegetable vendor with big avocados
on the way to Aguas Buenas in Puerto Rico

53

Stuffed avocado
Relleno de Aguacate

---

1 lb shelled deveined, medium size shrimp
2 tablespoons finely chopped onion
2 large eggs, hard-boiled and finely chopped
2 tablespoons drained brine packed Spanish capers. (optional)
2/3 cup mayonnaise
2 tablespoons tomato paste or ketchup
1/4 teaspoon Spanish or mild paprika
1 tablespoon chopped fresh parsley
Salt and freshly ground black pepper to taste
3 medium size ripe avocados, with pit removed, sliced in half with skin left on, and a small slice cut off the bottom of each half to enable the fruit to sit steadily on the plate.
Salad greens to line the plates
1 pimiento, finely chopped for garnish.

In a sauce pan filled with just enough warm water to cover the shrimp, put in the shrimp then boil for 3 minutes, drain well and cut into thirds.

In a large bowl, combine the shrimp, onion, eggs and capers. In a small bowl, mix the mayonnaise, tomato paste, paprika, and parsley, pour the mixture over the shrimp, and toss lightly to mix. Season with salt and pepper and refrigerate until ready to serve.

Place each avocado half on a plate lined with salad greens, mound with the shrimp salad, garnish with the pimiento, and serve.

Makes 6 servings

SANDWICHES

CUBAN SANDWICH
SANWICH CUBANO

1 Loaf Cuban or Italian bread
2 tablespoons mayonnaise
2 slice swiss cheese
4 ounces sliced roast pork
4 ounces sliced boiled or baked ham
2 small dill pickles thinly sliced lengthwise.
1 tablespoon butter, melted

Preheat the oven to 350 degrees F.

Slice the bread in half lengthwise. Spread both cut surfaces with mayonnaise, layer one half with pickle slices, cheese, pork, and ham, cover with the second slice of bread, and cut down the middle into two sandwiches.

Place the sandwiches on a lightly oiled baking sheet and brush the tops with butter. Place a heavy cast-iron skillet over both sandwiches to weigh them down, and bake until crisp and hot, about 10 minutes.

Makes 2 sandwiches

Here is Dolores going on a tour in Puerto Rico

The rise and fall of Doll 's Kitchen

The year was 1999, Dolores (Doll) Batista and I had been dating for a few months when she invited me to a musical concert at Hotos community college, On that same evening Lydia one of Dolores friends was celebrating her birthday. Doll wanted to invite the group attending the concert to the house for drinks and asked me to prepare a few snacks to munch on after the concert. Since there were about 15 friends invited 1 prepared 20 different items, chicken, shrimp, salmon, beef, vegetables, dips and six different salads. I started about three that afternoon and was finished by 6 P.M . We left for the concert around 7 P.M. Dolores was concerned that my extended effort would be a waste of time. She said, honey I know my friends and its going to be late in the evening when we get home and they are not going to be hungry. What I usually do is open a bag of chips and pretzels, buy some wine and that's it. Well I was never the chips and pretzel kind of guy. The concert was excellent and was about to end around 9 P.M. before the last musical number started I whispered to Dolores that I was going ahead to set up the table so that everything would be ready. When our guest arrived our big table was set up with a floral arrangement in the center. You had to be there, for no sooner did the coats came off that it looked like Kmart was having a free shopping day as the food quickly disappeared, a hush came over the room and all that was heard was the MMMMMs sound. Soon after the small feast was over, Gus, one of our friend came over and pointed to the sign on the kitchen that reads La Cocina De Dolly. Doll he said, we have to change the name on that sign to read La Cocina de Julio. To which Dolores replied "30 years I have cooked for you guys and one night of Julio's cooking and you drop me like a hot potato" We all got a good laugh as they crossed of her name and inserted in mine. Six wonderful years have past and it's still Doll's Kitchen, although Dolores doesn't cook much since 1 became resident chef

The other day I asked Dolores if she wanted to go somewhere she hasn't been to in a while, (she thought to was talking about a vacation) I pointed to the kitchen. That evening we had dinner out and Dolores made her favorite dish "reservations ". I didn't mind much, I got to eat what I wanted and Dolores picked up the tab.

STEAK SANDWICH

Hero bread
Mayonnaise
Onions
Lettuce
Tomato slices
Crushed garlic in olive oil
Cubed steak
2 Tablespoons olive oil

Hispanics love a good steak sandwich and who wouldn't? Especially if it's made right. Follow this recipe and that ham and cheese will quickly become your second choice.

Take hero bread and toast it until golden brown. Heat a frying pan at medium high and add 2 tablespoons of olive oil, fry the cubed steak to your preference, add the onions and fry them lightly, 2 minutes max, add mayonnaise to both ends of the toasted bread, put the steak and onions on the toasted bread add the onions on top of the steak and follow with the lettuce and tomatoes, now drizzle with garlic and olive oil mixture, cut in half and sink your teeth into a hot delicious steak sandwich, followed by your favorite beverage, "YES" sandwich heaven.

ROAST PORK SANDWICH
SANDWICH DE PERNIL

Hero Bread / sliced
Mayonnaise on each slice
Sliced roasted pork (pernil)
Olive oil with crushed garlic, drizzle on top of the roast pork
A piece of the pernil (pork) skin on the top

The year was 1999 Dolores and I decide to have a New Year's Eve party. The Christmas tree was still up and there were gifts under it that needed to be delivered, so we thought this would be a good way to have our friends over and give them there gifts and at the same time have a New Years Eve party.

I went shopping for wines, champagne and other brands of alcohol plus to the super market for our late night feast. We had 12 different items to choose from for dinner, soup arroz con gandules, pork shoulder, chicken, shrimps, pasteles, bacalao, stuff mushrooms, potatoes, vegetables, cold salads, dips, cheeses, fruits, nuts and an assortment of desserts. Two bars were set up and we had all sorts of sodas, juices and even two types of egg nogs. The Charanga music filled the room and all the instruments for our musical guest to play with were in place. We call them (La Banda Barata).

Around 9P.M. our invited guest started to arrive and were greeted at the door by me and my camera, I must have taken over a hundred shots that night. The party was held in both floors and there was champagne everywhere. Soon the dancing started and La Banda Barata was playing, Ms Alicia Moreno was leading the group and we had several dancers performing. The joy and laughter was memorable after every musical number. The party continued until before midnight, when we stopped to give thanks and to reflect on the last year, and how lucky we were to have such wonderful friends to celebrate with. The usual hugs and kisses followed at midnight and the party rolled on until around 4A.M. Some people complained when we told them that the party was over, they didn't want it to end. We served coffee and long goodbyes as the morning chill filled the air on January 1st. For the next two weeks we received calls from friends saying what a wonderful time they had and that it was the best party ever.

You would think that after a bash like the one we had things would quiet down but nooooo, for around the 15th of January Dolores calls me at work, "Honnnney", whenever Dolores calls me with the long honey I know she wants something. Six of my friends from California are in town and they missed the party, can we have them over for a small dinner party this weekend. My first thought was, the floor isn't cold yet from the last party. I said yes and hung up the phone but I knew there was more to this then met the eye, and boy was I right for 2 hours later the phone rings again, "Honnnney, " oh, oh, was my first thought, what is it now?, I asked, knowing full well that it was about the dinner party. I think your going to have to go shopping for food, and wine, came her reply, I spoke to a few other friends and they want to come by too. As the day went by the 6 friends had grown to 20 and by the time the small dinner party was set to begin, there were 40 guest scheduled. I started the food preparation and of course we couldn't serve the same old thing so I prepared lamb as the main course along with 11 other new items. We called in la Banda Barata, and would you believe the second party was just as good if not better than the first. Our California friends had a wonderful time, but our poor living room floor had to be renovated from all the dancing.

EGGS

You can have eggs for breakfast, lunch, dinner, as a snack, a main course or a simple sandwich. The egg is still a great buy and a simple way to liven up a meal. On Sunday mornings, at Dolls kitchen, the egg is the star as we prepare brunch.

2 to 3 eggs
2 tablespoons milk or water
A pinch of salt and pepper
1 tablespoon of oil or butter

Scrambled eggs: There are various pans you can use, a nonstick sauté pan or aluminum frying pan. First preheat the pan, eggs will stick to most pans if the pan is cold or warm.

hint; poking the center of the yolk with a fork will make mixing easier and faster.

In a bowl lets crack 2 to 3 eggs, throw out the shells, add 2 tablespoons of water or milk, a pinch of salt and pepper and whisk until the mixture is scrambled.

Add butter or oil the pan, pour the egg mixture into the pan and stir constantly with a wooden spatula. Eggs are done when most of the moisture is absorbed into the egg mix, do not overcook. Eggs will become rubbery if you allow to stand too long after serving.

FRIED EGG OR EASY OVER
JUEVO FRITO

Frying: Make sure your pan is hot then add 1 tablespoon of vegetable or corn oil or butter. Slide the egg from a bowl, or directly from the shell onto pan, fry over medium heat for 2 to 3 minutes spooning the oil over the eggs or turn the eggs over, being careful not to break the yolk.

SOFT OR HARD BOILED EGGS

Remove eggs from the refrigerator and allow them time to warm up to room temperature.

(Cold eggs will crack when put into hot water)

Boil approximately 1 quart of water

With a slotted spoon put eggs in the hot water, allow 4 minutes for soft boiled, 10 minutes for hard boiled. Lift the egg, again using a slotted spoon, and put eggs in cold water, peel off the shell and put back in water to cool.

POACHED EGG

Bring to a boil a water filled sauce pan, add a pinch of salt, turn the heat down to simmer, gently add the egg (without shell) poach uncovered for 2 to 3 minutes, lift the egg out with a slotted spoon. Serve on top of toasted bread or English muffin.

EGG SALAD

4 Egg per serving, hard boiled and chopped
1 tablespoon finely chopped celery
1 tablespoon finely chopped onion or scallion
1 tablespoon mustard
2 or 3 tablespoons mayonnaise
Salt and pepper to taste

Mix well in a bowl

Serves 2 or 3 as a sandwich or side dish

Omelets
TORTILLA

Omelets are for Breakfast, lunch or dinner they are very simple to prepare. What you can add to fill an omelet is endless.

3 eggs is the most popular.
2 tablespoon of cold water
Salt and pepper
Small amount (pat)of butter

Combine eggs, and ingredients in a bowl then pour mixture into a pre heated buttered non stick pan, stirring gently, at medium heat with a wooden spoon/spatula.

SPANISH OMELET
TORTILLA

3 Eggs
2 tablespoons olive oil
1 onion sliced
1 Pepper, green, red, yellow, orange, whatever color pepper you have available.
1 sprig cilantro
1/3 cup tomato sauce
1 garlic clove
¼ teaspoon each of salt and pepper
1 Potato sliced thin

Boil water in a sauce pan and cook the potatoes until done, drain and allow to cool

Preheat a pan at medium heat and add 2 tablespoons of olive oil toss in onions, garlic,

Peppers, cilantro and sauté for 5 minutes stirring constantly then add the potatoes and tomato sauce cook for another 2 minutes uncovered and remove from heat.

In a sauté or frying pan make a scrambled egg omelet

Put 2 large spoons of the potato, onion and pepper mix to ½ of the omelet and cover with the other half. Lower heat and cook for 1 or 2 minutes.

Serve onto plates and spoon some of the mix on top.

Western Omelet

3 eggs, mix in a bowl
2 tablespoons cold water
Pinch of salt
Pinch of pepper
2 ham slices, chopped
¼ green pepper
¼ red pepper
½ small onion, chopped
1 pat of butter
2 tablespoons olive oil

In a preheated non stick pan add olive oil and sauté the ham, peppers and onion 3 to 5 minutes, stirring constantly. Remove from heat and separate, clean the pan, and preheat again, this time add the butter and the egg mix, then quickly add the ham, pepper and onion mix cook at low heat for 2 to 3 minutes, fold over and you are done.

Cheese can be added if you wish before the fold.

Other variations: Bacon bits, mushroom, cheese, salmon, shrimps, roasted pepper, potatoes, onions.

CHEESE SOUFFLES

¼ cup sifted all purpose flour
1 to1 ¼ cup hot milk
1 ¼ cup of grated cheese
1 teaspoon mustard
Dash of salt and pepper
4 large or jumbo eggs

Separate the yolks in one bowl and whites in another.

In a sauce pan melt the butter over medium heat, sprinkle in the flour while whisking for 2 minutes. Remove from heat and slowly add hot milk, whisking constantly, return to heat and continue blending until the sauce is boiling and thickened. Remove from heat add the cheese and stir until melted, add mustard and pepper.

Let cool then beat in the egg yolks. Whisk the egg whites in a separate bowl with an electric mixer until stiff. Whisk 2 spoons of the white egg mix into the sauce, and gently fold in the remaining mix. Spoon the mix into a large remakin then bake for about 15 minutes or until soufflé rises and is golden brown. *Never open oven door and then allow it to shut hard, the noise can cause the soufflé to fall in center.

STOCKS

FISH STOCK
CALDO DE PESCADO

2 to 3 lbs of fish trimmings (no skins, can be the bones or the head)
2 quarts water
½ teaspoons salt
2 large ripe tomatoes, cubed
4 to 5 cloves garlic, crushed
6 black peppercorns
1 bay leaf
1 large onion, quartered
1 large green bell pepper, seeded and cut into strips
4 or 5 strips of fresh parsley

Place all the ingredients in a large stockpot and bring to a boil over medium high heat, skimming any scum that accumulates. Reduce heat to low and simmer, partially covered, 30 minutes.

Remove from the heat and allow to cool. Strain the stock through a fine strainer. The stock will keep in the refrigerator 1 to 2 days and can be frozen.

GRANDMA'S FISH SOUP
POTAJE PESCADO

1/3 cup pure Spanish olive oil
I large Spanish onion, quartered
4 cloves garlic, crushed
2 large ripe tomatoes, chopped
10 sprigs fresh parsley
1/2 teaspoon ground cumin
3 large all purpose potatoes, peeled and chopped
1 teaspoon salt
Few dashes of Tabasco sauce
2 lbs firm fish (cod or sole,) fillets, tied in cheesecloth
Juice of' 1 lime
2 quarts of fish stock or clam juice
1 lime cut into wedge

In a large casserole, heat the oil over low heat, then cook the onion, stirring, until tender about 5 minutes. Add the garlic and tomatoes and cook, stirring, 10 minutes. Add the remaining ingredients, except the lime, bring to a boil, cover, and simmer over low heat for 30 minutes, until potatoes are tender.

Remove the fish with a slotted spoon and allow to cool, remove the fish from the cheesecloth and separate into small pieces. Place the pieces back in the soup.

Garnish with fresh chopped parsley and add the lime juice.

BEEF STOCK
CALDO DE RES

1 lb flank steak, cut into chunks
2 lbs beef bones
3 quarts water
1 ½ teaspoons salt
1 teaspoon black pepper

4 cloves garlic, crushed
1 bay leaf
1 large onion, quartered
1 large green bell pepper, seeded and quartered
4 or 5 sprigs fresh parsley
3 large ripe tomatoes, quartered
½ teaspoon ground cumin
¼ teaspoon powdered saffron, or bijol

Place all ingredients in a large stockpot and bring to a boil over medium high heat, skimming the scum from the surface until no more appears. Reduce the heat to low and simmer, partially covered, until the meat falls apart, 1/12 to 2 hours.

Remove from the heat and cool to room temperature, skimming any fat that rises to the surface. Remove the meat and bones then strain the stock through a colander, pushing down on the solids to extract the stock, and refrigerate or freeze for later use.

CHICKEN STOCK
CALDO DE POLLO

1- 5 to 6 lb fowl, quartered, including the giblets
3 quarts water
1 ½ teaspoons salt
½ teaspoon ground cumin
6 black peppercorns, crushed
4 to 5 cloves garlic, crushed
¼ teaspoon powdered saffron or 3 to 4 saffron threads, crushed
2 bay leaves
1 large onion quartered
4 to 5 sprigs of fresh parsley
2 ripe plum tomatoes or 1 large ripe tomato, quartered

Place all the ingredients in a large stockpot and bring to a boil over medium high heat, skimming the scum from the surface until no more appears. Reduce the heat to low and simmer, partially covered, 1 hour.

Remove from the heat and cool to room temperature, skimming any fat that rises to the surface. Remove the meat and bones then strain the stock through a colander, pushing down on the solids to extract the stock. The stock will keep in the refrigerator 2 to 3 days and can be frozen. Reserve the chicken for another use.

Makes 8 cups

Ms. Alicia Moreno, a special friend enjoying a glass of wine at our Bar B Que.

SOUPS/STEWS

After shopping in this market, I had the urge to run home and make Soncocho(stew)

My mother Gregoria Perez (god bless her soul) worked two jobs to make ends meet, she had no choice since there were 17 of us. I was the youngest and I remember going shopping with her to the neighborhood market near her job, we would shop for all kinds of vegetables and the kind butcher at the meat market would always give her soup bones so that moms could make her wonderful stock for our soup.

Sunday's was a day when the kitchen at our home would close early so that moms could get some rest and catch up on her novellas (soap operas). So on Sundays we had a large late breakfast and a soup or sancocho (stew) with white rice would follow late that afternoon. This practice was particularly true if was raining or snowing. Those two factors would guarantee that a big pot of soup or stew was on the menu for Sunday. My mother would say "on this cold day you need a meal that sticks to your ribs and warms your insides".

I would call her cooking "spirit food" as in "soul food ".

It was a pleasure to return home from the cold, the wonderful aroma would hit you as soon as you entered the door, and there was mom in the kitchen with a big smile, the table filled with all the vegetables she would use to create her sancocho.

Today my life is somewhat easier since I don't have to work two jobs or feed so many people but the lessons of my childhood still remain, because on rainy or snowy Sundays Dolores says that the first words out of my mouth upon waking are Sopa or Soncocho, Thanks Mom,

SANCOCHO

1-½ pounds top round beef, or short ribs cubed into 1-1/2 inch pieces
4 tablespoons olive oil
5 garlic cloves, minced
4 sprigs cilantro, chopped
1 teaspoon salt
1/2 teaspoon black pepper
3 quarts of water
2 beef boullion cubes
1 onion chopped
1 green pepper chopped
1/3 cup celery, chopped
1 medium size tomatoes, chopped
4 bay leaves
I teaspoon oregano
6 sweet chili peppers minced
2 green bananas, peeled and sliced into 2 inch pieces
1 lb. name cut into 3inch pieces
1 lb. pumpkin, peeled and cubed into 2 inch pieces
3 medium potatoes, quartered
1 large chayote, peeled, cored, and diced into 1 inch pieces (optional)
2 ears of corn, cut into 4 pieces each.

In a preheated kettle(large pot) over low to medium heat, add the olive oil ,beef, garlic, and onions, stir until beef is brown on all sides and onions begin to caramelize, next add the water, boullion cubes, chopped pepper, celery, sweet pepper, cilantro, tomatoes, bay leaves, oregano, salt, pepper, and stir, cook for approx 1 hour or until meat is soft, then add in all the remaining vegetables lower the heat and simmer for about ½ hour until the vegetables are done, and the soup thickens.

Serves 8 to 10

Since this soup contains beef and vegetables, it is hearty already. Serve alongside a bowl of rice or bread. This is another one of those soups that you should not have plans to go anywhere for a while after eating, except for a nap. You have been warned.

CHICK PEA SOUP WITH PIG FEET
SOPON DE GARBONZOS CON PATITAS DE CERDO

1 Lb garbanzos (chick peas) or 2 cans of garbanzos
If the garbanzos are dry they must be soaked in water overnight, then boiled for an hour or until tender. If they are canned they are added in the last ½ hour. (with the vegetables)
3 lbs pig's feet
**There are two types of pig's feet. Salted and unsalted. If you are cooking salted pig's feet, soak overnight in water, next day drain the water and add fresh water and boil, changing the water 3 times every ½ hour or until the salt is gone and pig's feet are tender. An alternate method is to buy unsalted pig's feet which are readily available in local stores, boil in water for 1 ½ hours or until tender. Now you can start cooking the pig's feet and garbanzos.
4 ½ quarts of water
2-lbs pumpkin, peeled and diced
2 chorizos (Spanish sausage), cut to one inch pieces
2 ounces lean cooking ham, washed and diced
1 green pepper, coarsely chopped
3 sweet chili peppers, seeded and coarsely chopped
4 fresh cilantro leaves coarsely chopped
1 onion peeled and coarsely chopped
2 cloves garlic, peeled and coarsely chopped
2 tablespoons of olive oil
½ cup tomato sauce
4 potatoes, peeled and diced
1 tomato, quartered
1 lbs cabbage, quartered
2 yautias peeled and cut into quarter pieces

In a heated frying pan add the olive oil, chorizos, 1 cup diced cooking ham, green pepper, 3 sweet chili peppers, onion, and garlic cloves, Sauté for 5 minutes at low/medium heat.

In a large pot with the pig's feet and garbanzos, add the tomato, potatoes, cabbage, yautia, pumpkin, Tomato sauce, cook at medium low (simmer) for 45 minutes to an hour until sauce thickens. Put in the cilantro at the end and adjust seasoning with salt and pepper to taste. If you wish you can add 2 additional tablespoons of olive oil for flavor.

Serve alongside white rice.

CLEAN THE REFRIGERATOR/HANGOVER/REHABILITATION SOUP

I call this soup the clean the refrigerator hangover rehabilitation soup because it's a perfect soup to make when the weekend is here and you are home wondering what to cook, and you're cleaning out the vegetable bin and soup comes to mind. This soup is really a vegetable soup, but the vegetables will depend on what you have in the box. There are times when you've been out dancing and drinking and you wake up the next day, like a part of your brain is missing, this is when you make this soup, but now it's called rehabilitation soup. You know the feeling, now let's make the soup. First look in the freezer, there's always a frozen piece of chicken somewhere in there, the chicken will add flavor to the soup, if you don't find chicken, beef bones work just fine.

1 Piece of chicken or beef bones
1 Chicken bullion cube or beef bullion cube depending on which soup you're making
2 Quarts of water
½ Teaspoon salt
½ Teaspoon pepper
1 Onion, chopped
1 Green pepper, chopped
2 Celery stalks, chopped
1 or 2 cloves of garlic, crushed

Cabbage, Carrots, Zucchini, Pumpkin, Tomato, Potatoes, or whatever vegetables you have on hand.

In a large heated pot filled with 2 quarts of water, add chicken or beef bones, add onions, green pepper, celery, salt and pepper, bullion cube, garlic, cook covered for 1 hour take the meat out and allow to cool. Remove meat from bones and put meat back in soup, add your vegetables continue cooking until tender. Add rice and/or noodles if you wish.

*Hangovers require plenty of liquids to replace the water missing in your system from the consumption of alcohol and a soup works just fine.

GARLIC SOUP
SOPA DE AJOS

This Mediterranean peasant soup is also a staple in Spanish Restaurants.

2 tablespoons pure Spanish olive oil
6 large garlic cloves mashed into a paste with 1 teaspoon salt
1 tablespoon of paprika
2 quarts of water
freshly ground black pepper to taste
5 large eggs, 1 of them lightly beaten
1 teaspoon finely chopped fresh parsley for garnish
1 old loaf of French or Italian bread cut into large cubes

In a large saucepan, heat the oil over very low heat until it is fragrant. Add the garlic and cook, stirring 1 minute, taking care that it does not brown. , add the water, and paprika, continue cooking for 5 minutes, add 1 beaten egg stir and cook for an additional 2 minutes, then add the remaining eggs (shelled) add them carefully so that they do not break, eggs will rise to the top as they poach, continue cooking for an additional 2 minutes, garnish with parsley and serve over 8 to10 cubes of bread in each bowl with one egg in each service.

CHICKEN VEGETABLE NOODLE SOUP
SOPA DE POLLO CON VEGETALES Y FIDEO

1 Whole 3 lb chicken washed and drained.
1 onion
1 green pepper
2 carrots, peeled cut into 1 inch pieces
¼ cup calabasa cubed (pumpkin)
2 large potatoes, cubed
3 garlic cloves, crushed
2 tablespoons sofrito mix
2 tablespoon olive oil
1 tablespoon salt
1 tablespoon ground black pepper
½ teaspoon bijol mix
2 chicken bullion cubes
½ lb of noodles

In a large pot heat 3 quarts of water to boil, add chicken and all the ingredients, cook at medium high heat for 1 hour, skim the fat scum off the surface as you go along. Turn the chicken several times to assure even cooking. After the hour turnoff the heat and remove the chicken, set aside to cool. After the chicken has cooled remove the meat and discard the bones. At this point you should decide whether you prefer cube chicken or you can shred the chicken into pieces. Put the chicken back into stock and start the fire again. Add ½ lb of your favorite noodles and continue heating for 10 minutes.

Garnish with chopped fresh parsley. Serve in large bowl with your favorite bread.

Makes 6 to 8 serving

Variations of above recipe

For vegetable soup: Follow the above recipe without the chicken or noodles, add whatever vegetables you wish.

For chicken vegetable soup without noodles, again same recipe, but no noodles.

For cream of chicken vegetable soup without noodles, same recipe. Add 2 cups heavy cream or half & half with 2 tablespoons corn starch in ½ cup of cold water.

CHICKEN SOUP WITH RICE
ASOPAO DE POLLO

1 whole chicken cut into pieces
2 sweet chili peppers
1 medium onions, peeled
½ teaspoon black pepper
2 tablespoon of sofrito
3 garlic cloves pressed
2 teaspoons salt
3 tablespoons olive oil
½ teaspoon oregano
½ cup tomato sauce
2 quarts water
1 red pepper, sliced
1 cup frozen sweet peas
1 chicken boullion cube

In a large soup pot put in the water, and chicken pieces, mix in all the remaining ingredients, except for the rice and peas, bring to a boil, cover and reduce the heat, simmer for 30 minutes. Rinse the rice under cold water, add rice to the pot, reduce the heat and cook uncovered for 20 minutes stirring occasionally. Add the peas and cook for an additional 5 minutes until the chicken soup thickens.

Serve in a large bowl with tostones or bread on the side.

GALICIAN BEAN SOUP
CALDO GALLEGO

1 lb Flank steak cut into chunks
1 lb cooking ham cut into chunks
2 all purpose potatoes peeled and diced
1 medium size onion, chopped
1 green pepper, chopped
4 small sweet green peppers (ajicitos)
3 mid sized chorizos cut into 1 inch pieces
½ lb of collard greens cut small
1 teaspoon salt
1 teaspoon black pepper
2 tablespoon olive oil
** 2 cans of northern white beans

In large pot boil 3 quarts of water, add the flank steak, ham, onions ,green peppers, salt, and pepper, bring to a medium heat ,cover pot and simmer for about 1 ½ hours. Add the chorizos, potatoes and collard greens cook for and additional 20 to 30 minutes add the canned beans and the olive oil and cook for 15 minutes, then cool for approx 10 minutes serve with French or Italian bread.

Serves 6 to 8

** If you prefer you may use dried white beans, soak ½ lb of dried beans, rinse them in cold water and let them soak overnight, cook them until tender about I hour then add them to the soup at the end.

THE CHICKEN/EL POLLO

The Chicken is my favorite bird for cooking, because of many reasons; first they are inexpensive and second, because of the varieties of ways they can be prepared. You can fry, sauté, stew, soup, fricassee, roast, bake, rotisserie, and Bar-B-Q. Chicken parts are used for other dishes, for example: liver and gizzards. There is a wide choice of birds; free range birds are usually the best flavored, corn fed have the best color, and frozen is good in value and less expensive. Chicken should have a light moist skin and a plumb breast; 3 to 4 lbs are the best.

Chicken wings along or with the breast are for pan frying, broiling or casseroles.

Whole chicken leg and thighs are for Bar-B-Q, pan frying, broiling and roasting.

Boneless chicken breasts, with or without skin, stuffed or not, pan fried, stir fried or broiled.

Chicken livers are great for broiling, pan frying, pates and sautéing.

Let's not forget grilled chicken in salads, and my favorite Arroz con Pollo.

STUFFED ROAST CHICKEN
POLLO RELLENO AL HORNO

1-5 lbs Roasting Chicken

Step One: Giblets, heart, liver, neck
1 Chopped onion
1 quart water
1 chicken bullion cube

In a 2 quart sauce pan cook giblets, heart, liver and neck for ½ hour remove chicken parts from water and allow to cool, save the water. Once cool remove chicken meat from neck bone and cut chicken meat, giblet, heart and liver into small pieces and set aside.

Step Two: Sofrito
2 tablespoons olive oil
2 strips of bacon, or cured ham, cut small
1 chopped onion
3 chili sweet peppers chopped.
1 green pepper
2 garlic cloves
1 stalk of celery cut into ½ inch pieces
6 pimiento olives, diced
6 slices of bread, cubed
1 apple, cubed
¼ of a stick of butter, melted
½ teaspoon of sage

Step Three: Stuffing mix

Preheat a frying pan, medium low put in the olive oil, fry 2 strips of bacon, onions garlic, peppers, garlic, celery, olives, and sage, stir until celery and onions are transparent. About 5 minutes. Add bread, butter, apple and the cut chicken parts and 2 cups of the chicken water to the mix. Blend and allow to cool.

Stuff chicken fully with stuffing mix

Put chicken into a shallow baking pan, add the remaining chicken stock, and ½ cup white wine, cover chicken with aluminum foil put chicken into a preheated 350 degree F oven.

Bake for 1-1/2 hour to 2 hours.

Basting:

   ½ teaspoon adobo
   2 or 3 sprigs of parsley, chopped
   ¼ lb of butter

Preheat pan, low heat, melt butter and add chopped parsley and adobo (or chicken seasoning) for basting the top of chicken. (approx. 4 times) Uncover aluminum foil and allow to continue baking an additional ½ hour or until golden brown.

CHICKEN FRICASSE
FRICASE DE POLLO

1-3lb chicken, cut into pieces
2 ounces of ham, dice fine
2 tbsp. olive oil
1 tbsp vinegar
1 medium onion, diced
2 carrots cut into 1 inch pieces
1 green pepper, diced
4 minced garlic cloves, or 2 tsp. minced garlic
1 tsp. dried oregano
2 sprigs of fresh cilantro, chopped
½ cup tomato sauce
1 bay leaf
12 stuffed olives
1 tsp capers
3 tsp, Adobo seasoning with pepper
2 medium potatoes, peeled and cut in ½ inch cubes
1Large can of sweet peas, drained, save the liquid for later.

Heat the oil in a pot over medium heat. Add the ham, and brown. Add the onion, pepper, garlic, oregano and cilantro, reduce heat to medium low and cook for 10 minutes, stirring occasionally. Add the chicken and cook on medium for 5 minutes, stirring occasionally. Stir in the tomato sauce, bay leaf, olives, capers, vinegar, adobo, carrots, and potatoes. Combine the liquid from the peas with water to equal 2 ½ cups, and add. Mix well. Bring to a boil, cover, reduce heat to low, and cook for 45 minutes until chicken is tender. Stir occasionally. Stir in the peas. Cook uncovered for 5 minutes or until sauce reaches desired consistency. Makes 6 to 8 servings

1 Chicken cut into large pieces
1 Large can of tomato sauce or puree
1 tomato, chopped
1 onion, chopped
1 green pepper, chopped
2 cilantro sprigs, chopped
½ tablespoon of oregano
½ tablespoon of basil
1 teaspoon salt
1 teaspoon black ground pepper
½ quart water
1 cup of dry red or white wine
8 to 10 pimiento stuffed olives
3 tablespoons of olive oil
4 tablespoons of parmisan cheese

In a large cooking pot or kettle add the water and chicken pieces bring to a boil then lower heat to simmer, cook covered for 15 minutes. Now add all the remaining ingredients except the cheese and cover and continue cooking "semi" uncovered for about 45 minutes.

When the chicken is tender, boil water in a large pot for the rigatoni.

When water is boiling add 1/2 teaspoon salt and 1 tablespoon of vegetable oil, add the rigatoni and cook for 5 minutes, don't overcook, drain pasta and put in with the chicken, blend in and continue cooking for another 5 minutes, add parmisan cheese while stirring, remove from heat, let cool 5 minutes and serve with Italian bread and a mixed salad.

As my children were growing up, this was their favorite dish; I couldn't stop them from eating less then 3 times each. The other day I made this dish and sure enough Dolores had an extra serving.

*Substitue. This dish can also be done by adding a jar of good Italian sauce to the mix instead of tomato puree and adding 2 tablespoons of sofito.

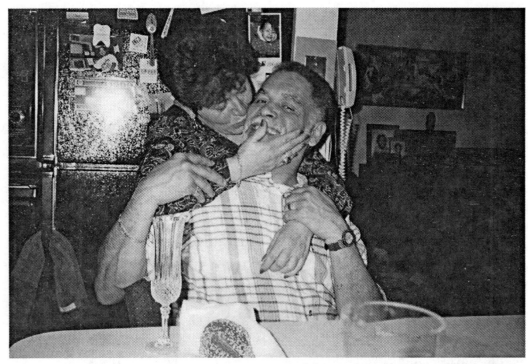

Dolores, Kiss, My reward for cooking

Angel and Ana enjoying the chicken at our Bar B Que

CHICKEN, FRIED AND STEAMED WITH WINE AND ONIONS
POLLO FRITO CON VINO Y CEBOLLA

This recipe is for you fried chicken lovers who worry about eating fried foods and are concerned about the oil content in the chicken. The recipe is original and I guarantee that once you try my fried/steamed wine chicken with onions you too will love and continue to prepare your fried chicken this way.

1 Chicken cut into pieces
1 Cup all purpose flour
1 Cup Buttermilk (regular milk will do)
½ Teaspoon black pepper
1 Teaspoon salt
½ Teaspoon oregano
1 Teaspoon garlic powder
½ Cup corn or vegetable oil
¼ Cup olive oil
½ Cup white wine
1 Large onion, sliced

Soak your chicken in the milk for 2 to 4 hours or overnight if you wish. In a bowl add the flour, salt, pepper, oregano and garlic powder, mix well, then take the chicken out from the milk and put into the flour mix, turn the chicken and coat all sides with flour. This process can also be done in a plastic bag.

Heat a large deep skillet frying pan at medium high heat and then add the oil, when the oil is nice and hot, carefully add the chicken, turning constantly, do not allow the chicken to stick to the pan, fry until golden brown, about 15 minutes. Now remove all the frying oil and add the olive oil, wine and onions on top of the chicken, lower heat to medium low, cover the pan and continue cooking the covered chicken for another 15 minutes remember to turn the chicken every 5 minutes and cover again. This process will steam the chicken and in 15 minutes you will have a delicious fried/steamed chicken with caramelized onions and a wine gravy that will have your friends asking "How did you make fried chicken so delicious?" and you can answer; buy "La Cocina de Dolly".

This recipe is best served with white or yellow rice or my favorite, mashed potatoes and buttered corn. Serves 6 to 8

FRIED CHICKEN MORSELS
MASITAS DE POLLO FRITO

2 1/2 To 3 Lbs boneless breast of chicken, cut into 1 ½ inch pieces.
Salt and freshly ground black pepper to taste.
3 cloves garlic, crushed
2 tablespoons olive oil
½ teaspoon dried oregano
½ teaspoon ground cumin
Juice of 2 limes
2/3 cup all purpose flour
1 teaspoon paprika
Vegetable or corn oil for frying
2 tablespoons finely chopped fresh parsley for garnish.

Wash the chicken, pat dry with paper towels, and season liberally with salt and pepper.

In a mortar, crush the garlic to a paste with the oregano, cumin, and olive oil rub the chicken pieces with the mixture. Place the chicken in a bowl and sprinkle with the lime juice. Cover and marinate in the refrigerator for 2 hours.

On a plate, combine the flour and paprika, roll the chicken pieces in the mixture to coat, and set aside.

In a large skillet, over medium high heat, heat 1 inch of oil until hot or until a small piece of chicken sizzles when it touches the oil, fry chicken pieces turning with a slotted spoon or tongs until golden and crisp, about 5 minutes on each side. Transfer the pieces to a paper towel lined plate.

Transfer to a serving platter, garnish with the parsley, and serve accompanied by the garlic sauce and your favorite rice dish.

JERK CHICKEN

Jerk chicken is a spicy blend of onion, garlic, thyme, nutmeg, cinnamon, and hot bonnet chili's. The jerk process originated in Jamaica as is used mostly for making jerk chicken and pork, grilled or baked. Jerk chicken and pork are Hot! Hot! Hot! So have a big glass of lemonade or iced ginger tea ready.

Jerk chicken marinade:

4 garlic cloves chopped
4 to 6 fresh scotch bonnet or habañero chili's, seeded and chopped
¼ cup fresh lime juice
2 tablespoons soy sauce
2 tablespoons olive oil
1 tablespoon salt
1 tablespoon brown sugar
1 tablespoon fresh thyme leaves
12 to 15 Peppercorns
½ teaspoon cinnamon
½ teaspoon nutmeg
2 teaspoon ground allspice

Blend all these ingredients in a blender until smooth

The Chicken

3 lbs chicken thighs and drumsticks
5 chicken breasts chopped in two pieces

In a large metal or plastic bowl, put in the chicken add the jerk marinade, blend well with a spoon, refrigerate overnight. Take out of the refrigerator and blend again, allow to stand at room temperature one hour.

GRILLED OR BAKED JERKED CHICKEN

If by grill, reduce fire to its lowest level, make sure the charcoals are gray in color, and grill chicken until brown on all sides move chicken away from charcoals and direct fire, cover with grill lid and grill for 30 minutes.

For baking arrange chicken in a roasting pan. Preheat oven to 350 degrees F. cover chicken with aluminum foil, poke 6 to 8 holes in foil with fork, this will allow steam to escape, bake for 45 to 60 minutes, remove foil continue baking until golden brown.

SMOTHERED CHICKEN
POLLO ESTOFADO

4 lb whole chicken, cut into serving pieces or 4 lbs large chicken pieces
1 can (8 ounces) tomato sauce
2 teaspoons salt
¼ cup olive oil
¼ cup vinegar
12 olives stuffed with pimientos
1 teaspoon capers
4 cloves garlic, peeled and crushed
1 onion, peeled and sliced
2 lbs potatoes, peeled and cubed
1 cup dry white wine or dry sherry

Wash chicken pieces and place in a Caldero or heavy kettle, together with ingredients.

Bring to a boil over high heat. Reduce heat to moderate, cover, and simmer for 1 hour.

Uncover, and simmer for about 30 minutes, or until chicken is done and sauce thickens.

What a wonderful holiday. I think it is my favorite because we celebrate with our friends and family. I remember as a child my mother would purchase a live 20 lb turkey in the first week of November, she would keep it tied up in the kitchen and fatten it up until the day before Thanksgiving, the turkey would now weigh 30 lbs. Through food we come together and share our love, our lives and with wine we toast to a better life and long lasting friendship. It is a wonderful day to have a good breakfast and then wait until its turkey time. Its also a holiday that if you are the cook you really need to start cooking the day before, because there is so much to do. Thanksgiving at Doll's Kitchen is a day filled a wonderful aroma as the turkey bakes slowly in the oven.

STUFFED ROAST TURKEY
PAVO RELLENO AL HORNO

10 or 12 Lb turkey
Wash turkey in and out and pat dry.

Seasoning:
6 cloves of garlic, peeled
12 peppercorns (whole black pepper)
1 teaspoon oregano
1 teaspoon salt
¼ cup olive oil
1 teaspoon vinegar

In a mortar, crush these items into a paste. Rub seasoning paste in and out of turkey; also don't forget under the breast skin. Under the breast skin insert small pieces of butter. Set into a large roasting pan and refrigerate overnight.

The Stuffing:

There are so many recipes for stuffing a turkey, Some Hispanic cooks use ground beef instead of bread, others add fruits, some add nuts, and they are all OK, whatever works for you is the right way. However since I'm writing this book, this is my recipe for stuffing the bird.

1 Loaf of bread cut into 2 inch pieces	*½ teaspoon pepper*
¼ lb. Butter (1 stick)	*½ teaspoon salt*
2 Celery stalks, chopped fine	*4 garlic cloves, crushed*
1 Onion, chopped fine	*1 Apple, cored, peeled and diced*
1 Green pepper, chopped	*¼ cup walnuts, chopped*
2 cups turkey stock	*2 tablespoons of olive oil*
Gizzard, liver, heart, and neck	*1 teaspoon oregano*
2 tablespoons ground or fresh sage (turkey stuffing seasoning)	

Preheat a sauce pan filled with 1 ½ quarts of water. Put in the neck, liver, gizzard and heart of the turkey, cook for about 1 hour at medium low heat. This will reduce to about 6 cups, of which 2 cups will go into the stuffing mix and the rest will become giblet gravy that you will make later on. After cooking set aside the neck, heart, liver and gizzard and allow to cool. Once cooled, take the meat from they neck and chop it along with the liver and heart and put into a bowl. These items will go in with the bread for the stuffing. The gizzard will be chopped and put into the remaining stock,

OK, now let's make the stuffing, Heat a large pan at medium heat and add the olive oil and butter, add the celery, onions, pepper, garlic cloves and cook while stirring for

5 minutes then transfer to the mixing bowl that contains the chopped turkey parts, add the bread, oregano, sage, apple, walnuts, and add 2 cups of turkey stock, mix well and stuff the turkey. You will probably have extra stuffing which you can bake for 1 hour in a separate baking pan, covered.

The turkey should be made ready for baking by putting it in a deep roasting pan, with 2 cups of dry white wine or water, orange, or pineapple juice, this will become part of your basting sauce and finally our gravy. Cover turkey with aluminum foil shinny side down.

Preheat the oven to 350 degrees F. and bake for 3 to 4 hours basting every ½ hour, uncover after 3 hours and remove the foil, continue cooking the turkey until golden brown. When you remove the turkey allow to cool for 20 minutes, strain the juices that are in the roasting pan into the two cups of turkey stock with the giblets, to make perfect giblet gravy.

* I know that the fruit juice part sounds a bit strange but try it and you will have a juicy sweet turkey

This is our Thanksgiving Day menu at Doll's Kitchen for 2007

Roast Turkey with apple walnut stuffing

Sweet giblet gravy
Arroz con gandules
Sweet baked potatoes
Potato salad
Fresh Cranberry sauce
Macaroni and cheese
Tossed green salad
Breads, and rolls
Deserts: Apple and Pumpkin pie with fresh whipped cream

Here are my children, Andre is on the left, and Justin on the right.
From Kids to adults and still enjoying Dad's cooking.

Making gravy is easy as 1, 2, 3,

So the next time you have a crust on the bottom of a pan or what appears burned on the bottom of a roaster pan, that's gravy! Well it will be.

Tilt the roasting or frying pan so the juice goes to the corner and remove most of the fatty oil. Leave the dark burn juices in the pan, bring the roasting or frying pan back on the heat, sprinkle 1 tablespoon of flour over the juices in the pan and whisk over medium heat for 3 minutes or until flour is absorbed and browns. Pour in 1 cup of stock, what's Stock? Take a heated sauce pan and add 1 cup of water and if you are making chicken gravy add ½ chicken bullion cube, if its beef add ½ beef cube, also add ½ cup dry white wine, and a pat of butter. Bring to a boil, whisking constantly, lower heat and simmer for 2 minutes then season with salt and pepper to taste and strain into a gravy dish.

Now put the stock into the roasting or frying pan, mix well and strain, Viola! You have gravy.

SEAFOOD

We had such a wonderful time last year visiting Puerto Rico during February, not just for the pleasure of leaving behind New York at its coldest time of the year. But is was my first time hanging out with our many friends who every year at this time venture forth to the island in search of warmth and relaxation. We stayed at our friends Gloria and Larry Cooperman's beautiful apartment near San Juan. We had arrived in Puerto Rico early to take advantage of our first day there and as soon as we unpacked we were off to the beach at Isla Verde to meet our friends. It is so wonderful to be in Puerto Rico during February, the weather is around 77 to 80 degrees and the beach waters are slightly warm that you can't help but feel somewhat guilty, but hey we're on vacation. We soon arrived at Isla Verde and were greeted by around 60 of our suntanned friends who had these beautiful happy faces and rum smiles. The Latin music filled the air and soon Dolores and I were dancing to the beat on the sand.

That afternoon we headed toward Piñones which is on the out skirts of San Juan and known for the best seafood on the island. We soon found ourselves driving through the main sandy road in Piñones looking for the right place to stop for lunch. We soon found a place that was about to open. Upon sitting and ordering two beers, I asked Dolores what type of seafood salad did she want. Conch, Shrimp, or Octopus to which she replied "all three" I ordered the salads and a (Chillo) Red Snapper for me, here is where I made my mistake, I didn't tell the waitress what size snapper. Dolores and I had just finished our three salads and we could have called it a day, when here comes our waitress with the biggest fried Red Snapper I've ever seen, plus rice, beans, tostones (fried plantains), lettuce and tomatoes. I looked at Dolores then at the Snapper for we knew we were headed back to the beach and could not take the fish with us. I glanced at Dolores once more, by now the young girl was apologizing and saying "you didn't tell me what size so I ordered the large. That day Dolores and I became little piggys, for we sat there ordered two more beers and proceeded to devour the red Snapper. We had to walk around and had trouble getting into our car and dinner was out of the question for that evening because we had it for lunch.

Some of our newyorican friends in Isla Verde in February enjoying the sun

Dolores walking on a sandy road in Piñones

Dolores and the three salads Conch, Shrimp, and Octopus

FISH TYPES

There are two types of fish: Oily and non-oily, below I have outlined the most popular.

OILY	*NON-OILY*
Salmon	*Cod*
Trout	*Haddock*
Mackerel	*Whiting*
Sardines	*Lemon Sole*
Kipper	*Flounder*
Tuna (fresh)	*Monkfish*
Carp	*Parrot Fish*
Anchovies	*Pollack*
Swordfish	*Red Fish*
Blue Fish	*Red Snapper*
	Sea Bass
	Tilapia

SHRIMP AND RICE SOUP
ASOPAO DE CAMARONES

Shrimp and rice soup is best made at home because I've ordered this dish in many restaurants and what I've gotten is hot water with 4 to 6 shrimps and rice in it.

NO SEAFOOD FLAVOR! Shrimp and rice soup is a wonderful flavorful dish when cooked the proper way, but it has to have a fine fish stock before hand, the recipe calls for a fish head and shrimp shells to be boiled. The shrimp shell contains most of the flavor, so remember that the next time you discard the shells, a little extra effort on your part by simply boiling the shells for 15 to 30 minutes, you can reduce the water stock to bring about better sauces if you are preparing shrimp in any other style. There is a product called clam base if you can find it buy it, 2 small teaspoons gives you perfect stock for a seafood sauce, soup or stews. When buying a fish head, discuss it with the fish monger, and make sure you buy a head that doesn't over power your finished product, stay away from oily fish. Go with the list provided on the prior page for guidance.

1 fish head (Cod, or Red Snapper etc)
1 lb. large shrimps, deveined, save the shells
1 cup rice, rinsed
1 green pepper, chopped
1 red pepper, chopped
1 medium onion chopped
6 sweet chili peppers chopped
2 sprigs cilantro chopped
1 medium tomato, chopped
4 garlic cloves crushed

2 tablespoons olive oil
1 tablespoon parsley
½ teaspoon Bijol food coloring
1 teaspoon salt
½ teaspoon black pepper
2 bay leaves
½ teaspoon oregano

Heat 2 quarts of water in a large pot, add the fish head and shrimp shells, boil at medium high heat for 30 minutes, remove and strain the fish stock making sure to remove all of the fish bones, <u>note</u>: If the fish head has some fish meat carefully and without the bones, put it back into the stock. Now add the stock back to the pot and add the salt, pepper, green and red pepper, onion, chili peppers, garlic, tomato, bay leaves, oregano, cook uncovered at medium heat for 3/4 hour, add rinsed rice, olive oil and cilantro, continue cooking for 20 minutes add shrimps, cook for 5 minutes allow to cool.

Serve with avocado slices in the soup. Serves 6

Having a bowl of shrimp rice soup will make you perspire a bit and you will not want to do anything but sit there, or maybe a nap for 30 minutes, but that's ok. You are going to like the way you feel, I guarantee it.

STUFFED RED SNAPPER
PARGO (CHILLO) RELLENO

5 Lb. Snapper, cleaned, remove back bone, head and tail; you can substitute Sea Bass, Red fish, Monk fish or Pike fish.
Juice of 2 Limes
2 Cloves of garlic, minced
½ teaspoon salt
½ teaspoon black pepper

Stuffing:
4 slices of bread cut into small pieces
2 tablespoons of olive oil
2 tablespoons of butter
½ cup of milk
1 green pepper, chopped fine
1 small tomato, chopped
2 garlic cloves, chopped fine
1 small onion, chopped fine
1 tablespoon parsley, chopped
pinch of salt and black pepper
¼ Lb. shrimp, shelled and deveined
1 teaspoon teriyaki sauce
¼ cup dry sherry
½ cup cooking ham, chopped fine
6 to 8 green seedless grapes(optional)

In a bowl, soak the bread, heat a frying pan at medium heat, add the oil, butter, onions, green pepper, tomato, garlic and ham, cook, stirring until the onions are soft, about 5 minutes, add the sherry, teriyaki and the parsley, mix and remove from heat, squeeze the bread and add along with the shrimps salt, pepper and mix well. Preheat oven to 375 degrees F stuff the fish then add the grapes transfer the fish to a shallow baking pan, and bake uncovered for about 1 hour, allow to cool, transfer to serving plate. Serves four.

CODFISH SALAD
SERENATA

1 lb. dried, unsalted codfish filets
2 onions peeled and sliced
2 tomatoes peeled and sliced
1cup olive oil
½ cup vinegar
¼ teaspoon ground pepper

Soak codfish in water for 4 hours. Drain well. Boil codfish water for 30 minutes. Drain and rinse in fresh water. Discard skin and bones, and shred the fish flesh.

Taste a piece of the fish to assure that the salt is out, if not, add water and boil again.

Arrange codfish on a platter. Garnish with onions and tomato slices.

Combine olive oil and vinegar to make a sauce. Pour sauce over fish, chill, and serve cold.

* The onions can be sauted in olive oil for 2 minutes if you wish to remove same of the sharpness in the taste.

This is a wonderful summer recipe to enjoy with white rice

Serves 6

Doll and the Newyorican snowbirds in Isla Verde San Juan, Puerto Rico in February.

1 lb. medium large shrimp
¼ cup olive oil
1 cup (2 sticks) butter
1 tablespoon parsley flakes
¾ teaspoon dry basil or 2 basil leaves
½ teaspoon oregano
¾ teaspoon garlic powder
¾ teaspoon salt
1 teaspoon fresh lemon juice

Peel and devien shrimp, leaving tails attached, split down the inside length wise, being careful not to cut through the shrimp. Spread open to simulate a butterfly. Place in shallow baking dish. Melt butter, add remaining ingredients and pour over shrimp. Bake in pre-heated very hot oven (450° F) for 5 minutes. Place under broiler 5 minutes or less until shrimp are flecked with brown.

Option 2: In a sauté pan add shrimps and ingredients sauté for 5 minutes turning once or twice, then place under broiler for 5 minutes or until shrimp are freckled with brown.

Serves 6 with Rice

SEAFOOD SALAD
ENSALADA DE MARISCOS

1 lb shelled and deveined medium-size shrimp cooked over medium-high heat in boiling, salted water and cover until pink, 3 minutes and drained well
1 lb cooked lobster meat, from 4 lobster tails simmered over medium heat in salted water and cover 5 minutes, meat taken from the shells and cut into thin slices or bite-size pieces.
1 lb cooked lump crabmeat
3 tablespoons finely chopped onion
3 tablespoons seeded and finely chopped green bell pepper
3 tablespoons finely chopped fresh parsley
2 tablespoons Spanish capers
½ cup chopped pimiento-stuffed green olives.
1/3 cup fresh lemon or lime juice
2/3 cup pure Spanish extra virgin olive oil
salt and freshly ground black pepper to taste
2 pimientos, finely chopped, for garnish
4 garlic cloves crushed

In a large bowl, lightly toss together the shrimp, lobster, crabmeat, onion, bell pepper, parsley, capers and olives.

In a small mixing bowl, whisk together the lemon juice and oil and pour it over the seafood. Add the salt, pepper and garlic, toss and mix, cover, and refrigerate for a few hours or over night, until ready to serve.

Line a large platter with watercress or lettuce and arrange the seafood salad on top, garnish with pimientos.

STUFFED FLOUNDER (LEMON SOLE) WITH CRAB MEAT

2 1Lb flounders
½ Lime
Pinch of salt and pepper
1 garlic clove, crushed
2 tablespoons of olive oil
½ stick of butter
1 stalk of celery, chopped fine
½ onion, chopped fine
½ green pepper, chopped fine
1 tablespoon parsley, chopped
¼ cup bread crumbs
1 can of crab meat
¼ teaspoon paprika

Wash flounder pat dry and squeeze on the juice of ½ a lime. Cut a line in center of flounder lengthwise, sprinkle salt and pepper, set aside.

In a heated frying pan at medium heat add oil, butter, celery, onion, pepper, garlic and stir for 5 minutes, allow to cool, then place in a bowl, add parsley, bread crumbs and crab meat, shape into a ball, place in a baking tray and put the flounder over it, like a hat, with the crab meat showing, sprinkle paprika, preheat oven at 375 degrees F. bake uncovered for 20 to 30 minutes. Serve and enjoy

*Note: this recipe is enough to make 2 servings of flounder with crab meat.

A great day of Fishing in Floria and I won the $65.00 pool with this red snapper

STEWED SHRIMPS
CAMARONES GUISADOS

2 lbs poached shrimps, shelled and deveined
1 teaspoon fresh lime juice
2 ounces lean cured ham, diced
1 teaspoon of bijol
2 cups of water
1 onion peeled and chopped
1 green pepper, seeded and chopped
3 sweet chili peppers seeded and chopped
2 cloves garlic peeled and chopped
6 fresh culantro leaves, chopped
1 lb potatoes, peeled and cubed
1 can (1 lb 12oz) of whole tomatoes
½ cup ketchup
6 olives, stuffed with pimientos
1 teaspoon capers
2 teaspoons salt
2 bay leaves.
2 tablespoon of olive oil

Heat a caldero or heavy kettle add the olive oil and rapidly brown the ham.

Reduce heat to low, add the bijol, onion, green pepper, chili peppers, garlic, culantro, and sauté for 10 minutes, stirring occasionally.

Add the potatoes, water, canned tomatoes with the liquid, ketchup, olives, capers, salt, bay leaves, and bring rapidly to a boil, reduce heat to moderate, cover and cook about 30 minutes, or until potatoes are fork tender.

Add shrimps and lime juice, mix, and cook, approx. 5 minutes uncovered, until sauce thickens.

Serve with rice as a side dish

Serves 6

SHRIMPS IN BEER
CAMARONES EN CERVEZA

2 Lbs shrimps, deveined but leave shells
2 cans of beer (10 oz. each)
1 tablespoon vegetable oil
2 ounces lean cured ham washed and dried
1 onion, peeled and chopped
1 green pepper, seeded and chopped
3 sweet chili peppers, seeded and chopped
2 cloves garlic, peeled and chopped
8 fresh culantro leaves, chopped
8 pimiento stuffed olives
1 teaspoon tiny capers
2 bay leaves
½ cup ketchup
1 lb potatoes, peeled and quartered

Wash well and drain shrimps. Carefully cut the shrimps on top and devein but leave the shells on for now. In a kettle, bring the beer rapidly to a boil.

Add shrimps, reduce heat to low, cover, and cook for 10 minutes. Remove from heat and allow shrimps to cool in the beer.

Drain shrimps and save the beer, remove shells

In a pre-heated caldero or heavy kettle, heat the oil, Rapidly brown the cured ham. Reduce heat to low and add the onion, pepper, sweet chili peppers, garlic, and culantro leaves for 10 minutes, stirring occasionally.

Add the olives, capers, bay leaves, ketchup and potatoes and the beer that was put aside. Bring rapidly to a boil. Reduce heat to moderate, cover, and cook about 20 minutes, or until potatoes are fork tender. Season to taste with salt and pepper.

Add shrimps, mix, and cook, uncovered, over moderate heat, until sauce thickens. Approx. 5 minutes.

Serves 6

FISH WITH GREEN SAUCE
PESCADO CON SALSA VERDE

Fish in a green sauce makes an eye popping display, baking a whole fish is easy to prepare and it comes out of the oven moist and tender. Start with a whole fish head and tail still on. Red Snapper is a favorite, but a red fish, striper, or sea bass work just fine.

One 5 or 6 Lb Red Snapper
Juice of 3 limes
Salt & Black pepper to taste
¼ cup of olive oil

The sauce
3 Garlic cloves, minced
½ cup of olive oil
1 bunch of parsley, chopped fine (no stems)
¼ cup of white vinegar
A pinch of salt and pepper
2 Tablespoons of Spanish capers
½ cup pimento stuffed green olives

Clean and pat the fish dry, cut slits on side of fish, pour lime juice in and out of fish.

Season with salt and pepper, cover and refrigerate for 1 hour. Preheat oven to 400 degrees F. place the fish in an aluminum foil lined baking pan, cover the tail with foil, sprinkle the fish with olive oil and bake uncovered for 1 hour. While the fish is baking prepare the green sauce. In a blender put the parsley, garlic, oil, vinegar, salt and pepper, blend until smooth, set aside. When the fish is done, take it out of the oven and carefully remove the outer skin then transfer the fish to a service dish. Next in a sauce pan heat at low flame, put in the green sauce and heat for 2 to 3 minutes then pour over the fish and garnish with the capers and pimento olives.

This sauce may be used for various fish dishes, for example: Shrimp, crab cakes, lobster, and scallops.

BOILED CRABS

1 Dozen live crabs

For making the stock:
2 quarts water
2 tablespoons olive oil
1 teaspoon fresh lime juice
1 ¼ teaspoon salt
3 fresh cilantro leaves
1 green pepper, seeded
1 tablespoon capers
1 onion cut quartered
6 olives, stuffed with pimientos
2 sweet chili peppers,

In a large Kettle with water and salt add the ingredients outlined above, and boil at medium heat for about 1 hour uncovered. What we are cooking is a stock in which we are going to add our crabs after they have been cooking in another pot with water for 15 minutes, (this is a cleaning process). Remove crabs from water allow them to cool, then separate the shell, and discard spongy tissue.

Add crabs to stock water and cook for 20 to 30 minutes.

Remove crabs from stock allow to cool, at this time they could be eaten as is. or add them to yellow rice to make Arroz con Jueyes (Rice with Crabs)

CRAB CAKES WITH GREEN ONIONS
FRITURA DE CANGREJO

1 egg, beaten
2 tablespoons of mayonnaise
2 tablespoons of minced green onion or scallions
½ teaspoon Old Bay seasoning
½ teaspoon hot red pepper sauce
1 lb lump or backfin crabmeat, drained and picked over for shells
4 teaspoons milk
1 cup cracker or bread crumbs
6 tablespoons olive oil for frying
lemon wedges for serving

Mix egg, mayonnaise, green onions, Old Bay and hot sauce in a small bowl until mayonnaise is completely incorporated then set aside. Lightly break up crabmeat in a medium bowl. Add milk and toss gently to coat. Add crumbs toss gently to combine. Add egg mixture, gently toss once again, to combine. Using a ½ cup measuring cup, scoop up a portion of crab mix, forming the mixture into a very compact cake. Repeat to make 8 cakes.

About 10 minutes before serving, heat oil in a 12 inch skillet over medium high heat. Carefully add crab cakes, sauté until golden brown on both sides, about 3 minutes per side. Transfer to a paper towel-lined plate. Serve immediately with lemon wedges.

OCTOPUS SALAD

1 Octopus of 2 to 3 lbs
2 to 3 quarts of water
1 green pepper, chopped
1 onion, chopped
1 tomato, chopped
2 garlic cloves crushed
1/2 cup olive oil,
¼ cup lemon or lime juice (fresh)
¼ cup vinegar
½ cup pimiento olives
1 tablespoon capers
1 tablespoon salt
½ tablespoon pepper
4 sprigs of cilantro
2 sprigs of parsley

In a large pot boil the octopus for 1 hour at medium heat until fork tender. Remove the octopus and allow to cool.

Remove the mouth from underside of the octopus.

Rinse and remove suction cups from tentacles.

Cut the octopus into 1 to 2 inch pieces.

In a large bowl mix the octopus with the other ingredients, blend well.

Allow to marinate overnight. Garnish with chopped parsley.

Serve with white rice or as an appetizer on a plate of lettuce.

BOILED LOBSTER
LANGOSTA HERVIDA

I've tasted many lobster dishes, and soaking a tasteless lobster in butter is okay, but I like a lobster to have more flavor. Recently I went to City Island for dinner with Dolores (Dolly). We ordered Shrimps and Lobsters for dinner. Both items tasted like paper, (tasteless) "No I'm not going to mention the restaurants name". I'm the kind of person that feels like, if I'm going to pay for a meal, I should get what I pay for and if I don't, I shouldn't have to pay for it; but I can't have that attitude when I'm out with Dolores, which is why most of our meals are made at home in Doll's kitchen. She says it's because I've been a chef so long. So to avoid having to send back food follow this recipe and stay home the next time you want to eat a really good lobster.

To make the stock

4 quarts of water
2 celery stalks
2 tablespoons salt
1 large onion quartered
6 crushed garlic cloves
1 green pepper quartered
12 to 15 peppercorns
2 tablespoons sofrito
1 tablespoon Adobo (optional)
4-1 ½ to 2 lb Lobsters
2 sticks (1/2 lb) of melted butter, for dipping lobster meat.

Put all the items in a large pot with exceptions to the butter and lobsters. Boil at medium high heat for about an hour. Taste the stock and make whatever adjustments to the flavor of the stock at this time. Now put in the lobsters in the pot of boiling stock but don't let your wife or date see this part (they get turned off). Boil the lobsters covered for about 15 to 20 minutes. Turn off the flame and be careful opening the lip off the pot.(steam will burn you) Take the lobsters out using a tong and allow them to cool before serving. Melt the butter and enjoy a delicious lobster dinner.

COCONUT SHRIMP WITH TAMARIND GINGER SAUCE

Making the sauce:

1 teaspoon tamarind concentrate or fresh tamarindos (no seeds)
1 ½ tablespoons honey
1 ½ tablespoons fresh lime juice
2 teaspoons Dijon mustard
2/3 cup mayonnaise
¼ teaspoon salt
1 teaspoon finely grated peeled fresh ginger

In a small bowl, whisk together tamarind and lime juice until tamarind is completely dissolved, now stir in the rest of the sauce ingredients and chill, covered.

For the shrimp:

1 cup all purpose flour
4 cups sweetened flaked coconut (10 oz) chopped
1 teaspoon baking soda
1 cup beer
5 cups vegetable oil
1 large egg
1 teaspoon cayenne
½ teaspoon salt
40 medium shrimp in shell (1 ½ lb), deveined, peeled, leaving tail and first segment of shell intact,

Transfer ½ of coconut to a shallow bowl. Whisk together flour, beer, baking soda, eggs, salt, cayenne, and egg in a small bowl until smooth. Heat oil in a 4 to 6 quart deep heavy pot over moderately high heat to 350 degrees F. While oil is heating, coat shrimp, Hold one shrimp by tail and dip into batter, letting excess drip off, then dredge in coconut, coating completely and pressing gently to help adhere. Transfer to a plate and coat remaining shrimp in same fashion, adding remaining coconut to bowl as needed. Fry shrimp in oil in batches of 8, turning once until golden (about 1 minute). Using a slotted spoon transfer the shrimp to paper towels let drain and season lightly with salt.

Skim any coconut from oil and return oil to 350 degrees F between batches.

Serve the shrimp with sauce, serves 8.

PAELLA

2 lbs chicken pieces
Juice of 1 fresh lime
¼ cup olive oil
2 teaspoons salt
2 quarts water

1 lb frozen lobster tail meat, without shells
12 mussels,
12 clams
2 lbs raw shrimp, medium size and deveined.
2 tablespoons salt
Juice of 1 fresh lime

2 chorizos (Spanish sausage) cut in pieces
2 green peppers, seeded and finely chopped
2 onions, peeled and finely chopped
2 tomatoes, finely chopped
6 large cloves garlic, peeled and finely chopped
½ teaspoon saffron threads
2 tablespoons paprika

4 cups long grain rice
1 cup of white wine

1 can (7 oz) pimientos
1 small can of green peas

Cut chicken pieces in half, wash, dry, and season with salt and lime juice.

In a preheated caldero, add ¼ cup olive oil and the chicken pieces, sauté frying for 10 minutes, stirring constantly, do not allow chicken to stick to bottom of caldero. After 10 minutes take the chicken out and set aside. To the same caldero add onions, green peppers, tomatoes, garlic, and chorizo, sauté fry for 10 minutes at medium low heat, add precooked chicken, paprika, saffron and 2 quarts water, cook for 30 minutes or until chicken is tender. Rinse the rice and add to the chicken, make sure that the water is 1 inch above the rice, cook uncovered for 15 minutes at medium heat.   When the water is absorbed, cover and lower heat to low continue cooking for 10 more minutes. At this time add 1 cup of white dry wine, the clams, lobster, mussels, shrimps, pimiento and peas. Transfer to a preheated oven of 350 degrees F. and bake for 15 to 20 minutes, the clams and mussels will open; remove any that do not open.   The shrimp will be cooked and the paella should be moist, you can always add an additional ½ cup of wine for moisture.

Paella is a lot of work but the final product is worth it. You should be able to feed up to 12 hungry mouths with the above recipe.

PICKLED FISH
PESCADO EN ESCABECHE

3 lbs Cod, haddock, or king fish slices, 2 inch thick
2 Cups olive oil
1 Cup Vinegar
12 peppercorns (whole black peppers)
½ teaspoon salt
2 bay leaves
4 onions peeled and sliced
Juice of 1 large lime
1 cup seasoned flour (salt & pepper)
2 large cloves garlic, peeled and crushed
12 Pimiento olives
1 Green roasted pepper

In a pre-heated large kettle, mix 1 cup olive oil, vinegar, 12 peppercorns, ½ teaspoon salt, bay leaves and onions. Cook over low heat for 15 minutes. Allow to cool.

Rinse fish in running water and dry. Sprinkle lime juice over the fish slices and flour both sides.

In a pre-heated frying pan, heat remaining olive oil and crushed garlic. Remove garlic as soon as it is brown

Add as many fish slices as will fit in the pan and brown over moderate heat on both sides. Remove the fish and place on paper towels.

In a deep glass dish, arrange the fish, onions, roasted peppers and pour the sauce over.

Cover and place in refrigerator for at least 24 hours before serving. Serve cold.

Serves 8

COD FISH FRITTERS
BACALAITOS FRITOS

½ lb dried salted fillet of codfish
1½ cups flour
¾ teaspoon salt
1teaspoon baking powder
1½ cups water
4 peppercorns (whole black peppers)
2 cloves garlic, peeled
3 fresh cilantro leaves
Crush and mix the peppercorn, garlic, and cilantro in a mortar & Pestle
Corn or vegetable oil for deep frying

Cut codfish into 2 inch pieces. Cover with water in a large pot and boil rapidly for 15 minutes.

Drain remove skin and bones from codfish. Rinse in fresh water two or three times.

Taste fish for salt content if salty, drain water reheat, repeat until all the salt is removed.

In a bowl, make a batter by blending ingredients and mix.

Add shredded codfish and mix thoroughly.

Drop mixture by spoonfuls in oil heated to 365 degrees F., until golden brown

Remove and drain, on paper towels.

Recipe yields approx. 30 bacalaitos

FISH STOCK
CALDO DE PESCADO

2 to 3 lbs of fish trimmings (no skins, can be the bones or the head)
2 quarts water
1½ teaspoons salt
2 large ripe tomatoes, cubed
4 to 5 cloves garlic, crushed
6 black peppercorns
1 bay leaf
1 large onion, quartered
1 large green bell pepper, seeded and cut into strips
4 or 5 strips of fresh parsley

Place all the ingredients in a large stockpot and bring to a boil over medium high heat, skimming any scum that accumulates. Reduce heat to low and simmer, partially covered, 30 minutes.

Remove from the heat and allow to cool. Strain the stock through a fine strainer. The stock will keep in the refrigerator 1 to 2 days and can be frozen.

GRANDMA'S FISH SOUP
POTAJE DE PESCADO

1/3 cup pure Spanish olive oil
1 large Spanish onion, quartered
4 cloves garlic, crushed
2 large ripe tomatoes, chopped
10 sprigs fresh parsley
½ teaspoon ground cumin
3 large all purpose potatoes, peeled and chopped
1 teaspoon salt
Few dashes of Tabasco sauce
2 lbs firm fish (cod or sole) fillets, tied in cheesecloth
Juice of 1 lime
2 quarts of fish stock or clam juice
1 lime cut into wedge

In a large casserole, heat the oil over low heat, then cook the onion, stirring, until tender about 5 minutes. Add the garlic and tomatoes and cook, stirring, 10 minutes. Add the remaining ingredients, except the lime, bring to a boil, cover, and simmer over low heat for 30 minutes, until potatoes are tender.

Remove the fish with a slotted spoon and allow to cool, remove the fish from the cheesecloth and separate into small pieces. Place the pieces back in the soup.

Garnish with fresh chopped parsley and add the lime juice.

POTATOES

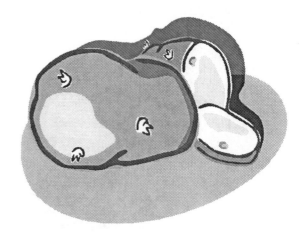

Potatoes come in many varieties and sizes. Thank goodness for the potato as a side dish, because there are so many wonderful things you can do with a potato. Some were developed by the Inca indians in Peru, by the year 200 BC Today the potato is best known mostly as a traditional Irish food due to the great immigration to the United States from Ireland during the Irish Potato famine of the 1840's. The part of the potato that we eat is the "tuber". The most popular potato today is the Russet, it is also known as the Idaho Baking potato. These potatoes are high in starch, and have light brown skin and white flesh, they are light and fluffy when cooked, baked or mashed, and they are also excellent in roasting or frying.

Potatoes are sold fresh, frozen, dehydrated, and canned, or as French fries. frozen potatoes are widely used, and let 's not forget the potato chip

Round white: Eastern round whites (all purpose) are available all year round, with medium starch and mash smooth, with a light tan skin. This potato is creamy in texture.

Long white, or White rose: (all purpose). The California potato is available in spring and summer. Long whites are oval in shape, medium starch, and thin light tan skin, with a firm creamy texture when cooked

Round red: These potatoes are available most in summer and early fall. The potatoes are small to medium in size with redskin. They have a firm yet smooth moist texture. Excellent in roasting, boiling salads and make good mashed

Yellow Yukon gold: Popular in Europe and the United States available late summer and early fall. They are dense yet creamy in texture, and their golden color has you thinking they are buttered when mashed. Excellent choice but expensive

Blue and Purple potatoes originated in South America and are becoming popular in the United States, most as snacks natural foods, and as chips these potatoes have a nutty flavor and the color is blue to lavender. I guess we have to get used to eating blue mashed potatoes

Dehydrated potato flakes and granules are okay in a pinch but they require water, milk butter and seasoning plus gravy to make them appetizing. Dehydrated potatoes also come in slices, shredded and diced, they make au gratin side dishes. Dehydration means that the water has been taken out, so soak these potatoes well before using.

Potatoes turn green when exposed to too much light, and they have a bitter taste. Store potatoes in a cool dark place with good ventilation, do not store with onions. Clean and trim any green areas before using.

Prepare potatoes whenever possible with the skin on for added nutrients.

Microwave potatoes: Dolores covers them wrapped in moist paper towels; they cook quickly this way, about 5 to 10 minutes depending on size.

Oven baked: Always heat oven first to 400 degrees F. There are various ways:

1. Rub oil on entire potato or
2. Cover with aluminum foil or
3. Pierce potato in several places so the steam can escape, bake until fork tender

Stove top preparation: Heat a saucepan with half filled warm water, then put in trimmed and cut potatoes, cook covered or uncovered about 10 to 15 minutes, or until tender, drain, use a potato masher to mash the potatoes; add milk butter and or mayonnaise with a pinch of salt and pepper

Frying potatoes: Peel and cut potatoes; and soak them in salted water, this process will do two things:

1. Keep your potatoes white and stops discoloring
2. it adds salt to the potatoes

Cut potatoes 1 inch wide for French fries

Cut potatoes 2 inches wide for Texas Fries

After soaking for 5 minutes, heat a pan at medium heat and add enough oil to cover the potatoes you are going to fry. Drain potatoes and place them on a paper towel if you are making Texas fries, over season the potatoes with salt and pepper, paprika and garlic powder. Put the potatoes into the hot oil, carefully to avoid splatter, put enough potatoes but do not overcrowd, too many potatoes and the oil will reduce in temperature and you will get oily potatoes. Fry until golden brown on both sides remove with a slotted spoon and place them on a paper towel

Roasted potatoes: Heat oven to 425 degrees F. put potatoes in tray, season, add olive oil and roast for 30 minutes, moving the potatoes occasionally, this will prevent them from sticking and burning

Hash browns: Preheat a pan at medium heat add olive oil and/or butter then add the shredded potatoes, cook until the bottom is golden brown and turn over to brown other side, season with salt and pepper.

Scalloped Potatoes
2 Lbs Potatoes
2 cups milk
1-1/2 cups heavy cream
1 large clove garlic, mashed
¾ teaspoon salt

½ teaspoon white pepper
1 tablespoon butter
½ cup grated Gruyere cheese

Peel potatoes and slice them 1/8 inch thick. Place in a large saucepan. Add milk, cream, garlic, salt and pepper. Heat to boiling stirring occasionally

Butter a gratin dish or shallow baking dish with 1 tablespoon butter. Spoon in potato mixture. Sprinkle with cheese. Bake in a preheated 400 degree oven for 45 minutes. Reduce heat to 350 degrees bake 30 minutes longer. Cover potatoes with foil if they become too brown. Let stand 5 minutes before serving.

POTATO SALAD

6 to 8 potatoes, skinned, cubed
2 to 4 carrots, skinned, cut into1 or 2 inch pieces
4 eggs, boiled and chopped
1 celery stalk, chopped fine
1 onion, chopped fine
4 tablespoons mayonnaise
1 tablespoon mustard
Season to taste, salt, pepper, garlic, oregano, adobo, parsley

Combine the potatoes, carrots, eggs, and boil until potatoes and carrots are tender (do not overcook). Discard the water after the boiling process.

Remove the shell from the eggs, chop the celery, and onions, cut into small pieces.

Put all the ingredients into a bowl, add mayonnaise, mustard, and season to taste

Garnish with parsley,

Serves 6 to 8

MASHED POTATOES

6 to 8 potatoes skinned and boiled until done
Strain, add salt and pepper
1 tablespoon butter
3 tablespoons mayonnaise

Mash the potatoes, add small amounts of milk if needed for proper consistency

Yields 6 to 8 servings

** For garlic mashed potatoes, Bake the garlic cloves, one clove per serving

HOME FRIED POTATOES

4 potatoes peeled, sliced or cubed
1 small onion chopped
1 small green pepper chopped
½ small tomato chopped
2 tablespoons vegetable oil or bacon oil
salt and pepper to taste
½ teaspoon of garlic powder
½ teaspoon paprika

Boil potatoes until almost done (check with a fork)

Drain potatoes and dry on paper towels, potatoes need to be as dry as possible for best results when frying.

Heat a frying pan at medium heat and add the oil or if you are frying bacon use 2 tablespoon of the bacon oil.

Add the potatoes, onion, tomato, pepper, and the spices. Allow the potatoes to fry until golden brown before turning them over. Fry on each side for about 5 minutes.

Serves 6

MORTAR AND PESTLE

Pilon

PILON (mortar and pestle)

Just about every Hispanic home has one or two mortar and pestles (pilon). Some people collect them. I've been to homes where the collection fills a counter top and growing. The mortar is a bowl shaped container made from hardwood, marble, pottery, ceramic, granite, volcanic rock or stone. The pestle is a tool used to grind inside the mortar (bowl) and pulverize grains, herbs, nuts into paste or powders, and other foods substances as well as for medicines. In our home the pilon is used mostly for large amounts of garlic, salt and pepper, (when making pork shoulder) pernil. Brief History of the Mortar and Pestle (Pilon)

Italians in the 15 Century used mortar and pestles by Apothecaries (ancient Pharmacists).

The Molcajete, or Mexican version of the mortar and pestle appears in Mexican prehistory as early as the discovery of the hybridized corn 6,000 years ago. Foods traditionally prepared includes salsas and guacamole. It's also for grinding chilies, garlic, herbs, and spices.

Many Mexican mortar and pestles are made from volcanic stone. The Thais (Thailand) use a stone granite mortar and pestle that dates back hundreds of years to the 13 Century AD. The mortar and pestle is used for grinding medicines, or ingredients used in thai cooking, seafood, fresh basils, palm sugar, lime, garlic, fresh ginger, tamarind, chilies and lemon grass. How to use it;

Place the items to be grounded inside the mortar (bowl). Sit the pestle on top of the substance and apply downward pressure, then grind using a circular motion. This action forces the substances against the surface of the bowl and pulverizes it. This grinding process releases the oils, and flavor essence of the substance. It is a laborious process so if your in a hurry reach for the food processor. If your mortar and pestle is made of wood, grinding food with moisture should be avoided as it will eventually cause the wood to split. Never soak a wood mortar in water, simply clean with a damp/dry cloth or paper towel and when dry add a small amount of oil to the bottom of the mortar and wipe, this process will help maintain your Pilon for a very long time.

A stone or volcanic mortar and pestle require prepping before using or you'll get grit in your food,

Wash and scrub the interior with a stiff brush, allow to air dry. Put a handful of uncooked rice in the mortar (bowl). Use the pestle and grind the rice in the mortar bowl. Discard the rice and repeat until the rice is white. Add 3 cloves of garlic (peeled), I teaspoon of cumin (comino) I teaspoon of salt (kosher is best) and a teaspoon of pepper. Grind the mixture around the interior of the mortar. Discard the mixture. Rinse with clear water and air dry, now you are ready to beat away.

PLANTAIN---PLATANO

GREEN/MADUROS

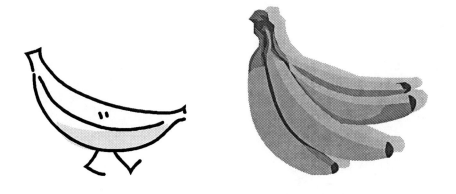

GREEN BANANAS---GUINEOS VERDE

PLATANOS

On a snowy morning in late November 2004, I mentioned to Dolores that we needed to shop for Thanksgiving dinner and the many pasteles that we had to make for Thanksgiving and Christmas and I wanted to show her a new super market in Bedford Park in the Bronx, that was owned by Hispanics and were having a grand opening.

As soon as we started out, Dolores looked at me and said; honey we have so many supermarkets in Throggs Neck, are you sure you want to go to Bedford Park on such a snowy day? I told her that I would take my time driving and that it would be worth the savings. And we proceeded on our slow careful drive. The snow had reached about 10 inches high when we arrived at the market. Dolores found the market to be really nice, and it had huge sales displays and marked down prices throughout the aisles, she was really surprised at the quality of the meat and produce departments and soon we were at the check out counter with a full carriage, that's when I remembered that we needed four platanos for the pasteles. Honey can you go to the produce section and get four platanos? Sure Dolores replied and she was off. Minutes passed and the cashier was about to complete the checkout, when I finally see Dolores slowly returning with her arms full of platanos, some were falling, some were held by her elbows, platanos everywhere! I looked at her, smiled and held up four fingers, four, and I repeated **FOUR.** Dolores finally made it to the counter. They were on sale fifteen (15) for a dollar, I couldn't let such a bargain go by she explained. But what am I to do with eleven additional platanos? We'll give them to our neighbors came the reply, late that afternoon I was out knocking on the neighbors doors and giving away platanos in a foot of snow.

MOFONGO

2 Green plantains
2 garlic cloves, crushed
2 tablespoons olive oil
Vegetable oil for frying
1 small bag of chicharron (pork rinds) crumbed or bacon

Mofongo is made by mashing tostones in a mortar (pilon), along with garlic, olive oil and chicharron

Peel the plantains, slice into 2 inch pieces, and fry in a preheated pan with vegetable oil over medium heat until tender, about 3 minutes on each side until golden brown

Remove from the oil and put on paper towels. After they have cooled down a bit, it's time to get a half of a paper bag, put a 2 inch piece of fried plantain in the middle, cover with the bag paper, and with the palm of your hand flatten it a bit. Repeat this procedure until all the plantains have been flattened out.

If you are using bacon, fry the bacon in a small amount of oil until crispy, cool and cut into bits. Now you can refry the tostones a second time, make sure your oil is hot you don't want soggy oily mofongo. Fry the tostones for about 3 more minutes, take out and put back on a paper towel.

Now we can make mofongo. Put from 6 to 8 tostones into a mortar (pilon) add the crushed garlic cloves and about ½ cup of the chicharron or bacon bits, and the olive oil, now mash the tostones, garlic and oil holding your hand over half of the mortar's opening while you are mashing, soon all the ingredients will be incorporated and you have a mofongo.

The mofongo can be served in various manners: as a ball surrounded by a nice stewed sauce, or in a well form and filled with stewed seafood. Try mussels, clams, shrimps or lobster, stew them all together for a grand mofongo, "Yummy"

*note: make sure to remove Shrimp skin and devein, also discard clam, mussel, and lobster shells.

FRIED SWEET PLANTAIN
PLATANOS MADUROS FRITOS

Soft in the center and crisp outside, these sweet morsels are my favorite way to enjoy plantains. Try them with any highly seasoned main course.

Ingredients:

Vegetable or corn oil for frying
3 medium size very ripe plantains peeled and sliced 1/2 inch thick diagonally.

In a large skillet over medium heat, heat 1 inch of oil to 375 degrees F., or until a plantain round sizzles when it touches the oil. Fry as many rounds as will fit in a single layer, until golden brown, 2 or 3 minutes for each side, turning with a slotted spoon. Drain on a paper towel lined platter and serve immediately.

TWICE FRIED GREEN PLANTAINS
TOSTONES

These crisp rounds are fried twice for extra crispness.

Tostones are a favorite side dish, they go with everything!

Meats, chicken, pork, soups, or by themselves as appetizers.

Ingredients:

Vegetable or corn oil for frying
3 medium size green plantains peeled, and sliced ¾ inch thick
Salt to taste

In a large skillet over medium high heat, heat 1 inch of oil to 375 degree F., or until a plantain round sizzles when it touches the oil. Fry as many rounds as will fit in a single layer until light brown, about 2 minutes for each side, turning with a slotted spoon, and drain on a paper towel lined platter. Set aside the skillet and the oil.

Fold a brown paper bag in half, place several plantain rounds between the halves and using the heel of your hand, soup can or mallet press down hard on the plantains until they are about ½ inch thick.

Return the tostones to the skillet, fry as many rounds as will fit in a single layer until golden brown, 3 to 4 minutes on each side, turning with a slotted spoon. Drain on a paper towel lined platter, sprinkle with salt, and serve immediately.

Serve with mojito garlic sauce.

Makes 6 servings

PICKLED GREEN BANANAS
GUINEITOS VERDES EN ESCABECHE

Escabeche sauce

   2 cups olive oil
   1 cup vinegar
   12 peppercorns (whole black peppers)
   ½ teaspoon salt
   2 bay leaves
   2 large onions, peeled and sliced
   2 cloves garlic, minced

   10 green bananas
   3 quarts water
   2 tablespoons salt

In a caldero or heavy kettle, mix ingredients except the bananas, water and 2 tbsp salt, and cook over low heat for ½ hour. Allow to cool.

Trim ends of bananas and slit just the peel, lengthwise. In a deep pot put in 3 quarts of water, 2 tablespoons salt, bring to a boil. Add the bananas make sure that the water covers the bananas. Cover and boil on low heat for 30 minutes. Drain, let bananas cool, and peel.

Cut bananas into 1 inch rounds. Place in a deep glass or porcelain dish, add the escabeche sauce. Refrigerate for 24 hours.

Serve as an appetizer

PLANTAIN SOUP
SOPA DE PLATANOS

1 ½ to 2 large green plantains peeled and cut into paper thin slices
Corn or vegetable oil for deep frying
6 cups beef stock or 6 cups of water and 1 beef bullion cube
1 Teaspoon salt, and 1/2 teaspoon of ground black pepper
Fresh lime juice to taste

Place the plantain slices in a large bowl, cover them with salted cold water, and soak for 30 minutes.

Drain the slices and pat dry with paper towels. In a frying pan or deep fryer, heat 2 to 3 inches of oil to 375 degrees F, or until a piece of plantain sizzles when it is put in. Fry the plantain chips a handful at a time, turning them with a slotted spoon until they are golden brown. Drain on paper towels. Do not fry too many chips at once, or the temperature of the oil will fall and the chips will be soggy rather than crisp. Using a mortar or a food processor fitted with a steel blade blend the plantain chips into a thick paste. In a large saucepan, heat the beef stock over medium heat. Gradually stir in the plantain paste blending thoroughly, and season.

Simmer over low heat, stirring frequently to prevent sticking, until the soup has thickened, 20 to 25 minutes. Serve hot, sprinkled with lime juice

Serve as appetizer to the main course. Makes 6 servings

RICE

GRAINS

Rice The most used grain of all. Store in a cool dry place, will hold well for 12 months.

WHITE RICE: long grain rice, an accompaniment to Rice and beans and other mostly main course dishes, separates when cooking, variable types of long grain.

BROWN RICE: Similar to white rice but longer cooking is required. Nutty in flavor with richness in vitamin, protein, and minerals, comes in short, medium and long grain.

INSTANT RICE: An alternative to white or brown rice. Grains are parboiled and never stick together, making it easy to cook. Medium and long grain are the most popular.

COUSCOUS: North African dishes are mostly accompanied by couscous. It really is not a grain it's a pasta.

CORNMEAL (POLENTA): A fine yellow grain made from corn, boiled in water, a staple in Italian cooking, can also be used for breakfast as a cereal.

FLOURS

In your quest to become a Pastry chef, start by buying flour in small bags, because most flours are best used in a 6 month period. Whole wheat flour tends to become rancid after 2 months especially during the summer months due to the heat.

WHITE FLOUR: An all purpose flour used for baking and as a thickening agent, also available as unbleached.

WHOLE WHEAT FLOUR: Whole wheat flour has a nutty texture and flavor and gives you a heavier result. I recommend sifting several times before use. After opening package store the whole wheat flour in the refrigerator.

BREAD FLOUR: This flour has higher gluten and is best used for baking bread. It produces a higher rise when making bread, available in white and whole grain.

CORNSTARCH: A fine flour made from corn, for thickening liquids, mix in cold water into a loose paste to avoid lumps.

CURRIED RICE

1 Medium onion, finely chopped
2 garlic cloves, finely chopped
3 tablespoons olive oil
2 tablespoons curry powder
2 cups long-grain white rice
1 quart water
2 teaspoons salt
1 teaspoon pepper
1 can coconut milk

Preheat a large sauce pan over medium heat, put in the oil, onion, and garlic, stir and cook for 5 minutes, add 1 quart of water, coconut milk, and curry powder, rinse rice and add to pan, season with salt and pepper, bring the heat up to medium high cook uncovered for 15 minutes or until water is absorbed by rice, stir rice cover and cook an additional 10 to 15 minutes.

Serves 8

Following the same steps for curried rice add a medley of frozen vegetables, peas, corn, string beans, thin sliced carrots, broccoli, and or zucchini. You decide what you want, in order to make you festive colorful Caribbean rice.

PERFECT WHITE RICE
(ARROZ BLANCO)

2 cups raw long-grain white rice or converted long-grain white rice
2 tablespoons pure Spanish olive oil (you may substitute corn oil or vegetable oil)
2 teaspoons salt
4 cups water if using long-grain white rice; 5 cups water if using converted rice

"Wash rice with running cold water"

Heat the water in a Large Pot (Caldero) add salt and oil, add rice to water, (the rice should be 1 inch under the level of the water) cook uncovered at medium high heat until the water has been absorbed and small craters form on top of the rice, 10 to 15 minutes. Stir the rice with a fork, cover, and reduce the heat to low, and cook until the rice is fluffy, 8 to 10 minutes. Fluff the rice with a fork and serve immediately.

* Dolores adds the oil first, then the rice. Stirred and then the water. This method is use by many housewives. So which ever way works for you it's o.k.

YELLOW RICE
ARROZ AMARILLO

For yellow rice we color the water with a condiment called bijol (a saffron substitute), or with crushed saffron threads or powdered crushed saffron. The simplest yellow rice is made using only rice and coloring; this enriched recipe has a touch of sofrito

(1 tablespoon per six servings) making it extra delicious as well as colorful. Yellow rice can be used wherever white rice is called for to accompany most Latin dishes, and Paella.

For the Sofrito:

¼ cup pure Spanish olive oil
2 cloves garlic, finely chopped
1 medium-size onion, finely chopped
1 small green bell pepper seeded and finely chopped.
1 cup drained and chopped canned whole tomatoes or 1 small can of tomato sauce
¼ cup dry sherry
¼ cup chopped drained pimientos
1 bay leaf

Put above ingredients into blender and blend until smooth, keep refrigerated. Or add them to a sauce pan as in the following recipe.

Yellow Rice continued;

2 cups raw long-grain white rice
4 cups water
1 teaspoons salt
½ teaspoon bijol or
¼ teaspoon powdered saffron, or 3 to 4 saffron threads crushed.
Freshly ground black pepper to taste

In a medium-size saucepan over low heat, heat the oil until fragrant, and then cook the garlic, onion, and bell pepper, stirring, until tender, 5 minutes. Add the tomatoes, sherry, pimientos, and bay leaf and cook 5 minutes. Raise the heat to high, add the rice, water, salt, and bijol, and cook uncovered over high heat until all the water has been absorbed and small craters appear on top of the rice, 10 to 15 minutes. Reduce the heat to low, stir with a fork, cover and cook until the rice is dry and fluffy, 10 to 15 minutes.

Makes 6 servings

YELLOW RICE ADD-ONS
ARROZ CON:

RICE WITH: Hispanic make rice with a variety of items, listed are a few choices.

- Vienna sausages (salchichas)
- Kernel corn
- Beans in the mix, any canned beans may be added to the rice: pinto, black, red kidney, chickpeas, in the first step after rinsing
- Arroz Moro (Black rice), 2 types with black beans or with canned squid.
- Cooking Ham (Jamon)
- Shrimp (Camarones), Boil shrimp shells first in seasoned water for 20 minutes, remove shells add rice to mixture and add shrimps 5 minutes before rice recipe is done (above)
- Seafood (paella), see recipe in the seafood section under (Paella)

RICE WITH PIGEON PEAS
ARROZ CON GANDULES

This rice deserves a page of it's own since it is the most popular rice that Hispanics make.

It is our signature rice for Weddings, Holidays, special occasions and at times our Sunday rice at mom's house.

The gandules can be fresh, dried, or canned.

If they are fresh cook them with a sofrito mix until tender.

If they are dry, soak them overnight then cook them with a sofrito mix until tender.

If you are using canned gandules put them in with the rice with the sofrito mix

Ok. Let's start.

¼ lb cooking ham cut into cubes
1 chorizo (Spanish sausage) cut to 1/2 inch slices
¼ cup cooking oil or olive oil
½ can Tomato sauce
½ green pepper
½ red pepper
1teaspoon adobo
2 garlic cloves, crushed
1 teaspoon bijol for color
2 tablespoons of sofrito mix
2 cans of gandules
salt and pepper to taste

In a large Kettle (Caldero) add the oil followed by the ham and chorizo, stir fry the ingredients for about 10 minutes add the green and red peppers, onion, and garlic, add salt and pepper to taste, stir and cook for 10 minutes, add the water, gandules, sofrito mix, adobo, tomato sauce, bijol, (remember the rico code; water, 1 inch above rice), heat uncovered at medium high heat for 10 to15 minutes or until the water is absorbed, stir rice lower heat and cover pot, continue cooking for 15 minutes, stir again and serve.

This recipe should yield from 8 to 10 servings of Arroz con gandules.

RICE WITH CHICKEN
ARROZ CON POLLO

2 cups uncooked rice, rinsed well
2 lb chicken parts, (dark meat has more flavor)
1 small can tomato sauce
¼ cup sofrito
1 tablespoon salt
2 tablespoons of sliced Spanish olives
1 teaspoon garlic powder
½ teaspoon black pepper
1 teaspoon capers
½ cup vegetable oil
4 cups boiling water
½ cup dry white wine
1 red pepper sliced

In large preheated cooking pot, (caldero) add oil and chicken, lightly brown the chicken on all sides, now add the water, tomato sauce, sofrito, salt, pepper, garlic powder, oil, and red pepper bring to a boil and stew for ½ hour at medium high , at this point the chicken should be half cook, now add the rice (remember the 1 inch above the rice rule) and all the remaining items, cook uncovered for 10 to 15 minutes lower heat to low, stir rice and chicken, over and continue cooking for 15 to 20 minutes, stir again add ¼ cup frozen peas and 1 tablespoon parsley, fresh or dry.

Serves 6

BEANS/LEGUMES

PUERTO RICAN CHICK PEAS
GARBANZOS CRIOLLOS

1 Lb. Chick Peas (garbanzos)
2 quarts of water
1 tablespoon Salt

First pick over chick peas discarding any foreign particles, like small rocks, then soak overnight, the next day drain the water and add fresh water and salt, put pot on medium heat and cook covered for 1 hour stirring every 20 minutes with a large spoon.

Sofrito :

1 teaspoon vegetable oil
1 ounce fried cut bacon washed and diced
1 ounce lean cured ham washed and diced
1 onion, peeled and cut into small pieces
1 green pepper, cut into small pieces
3 sweet chili peppers, seeded and chopped
2 cloves garlic, peeled and chopped
6 fresh cilantro leaves
¼ teaspoon dried oregano

Make the sofrito in a separate frying pan add to the pot of garbanzos and continue cooking until tender, about 30 to 40 minutes. Serve with rice or enjoy a bowl of chick peas all by themselves.

- Alternate method: You can always make the sofrito and add 2 cans of garbanzos, simmer for 30 or 40 minutes and your done.

RED OR PINK BEANS
FIJOLES COLORADOS

Pinto or red kidney beans are the basic ingredient for making "Congri" the popular Cuban dish for rice and red beans mix.

1 Lb dried red kidney or pink beans
3 quarts water
2 bay leaves

For the sofrito:

¼ cup pure Spanish olive oil
¼ cup bacon, cut thick and diced
4 garlic cloves
1 large onion, chopped fine
1 medium size green bell pepper, chopped fine
1 tablespoon vinegar
½ teaspoon oregano
½ cup dry white sherry
½ teaspoon salt
½ teaspoon ground black pepper
1 small can of tomato sauce

Soak the beans overnight. The next day, change the water, put the beans in a large pot with enough water to cover the beans, add the bay leaves and bring to a boil then lower the heat to a simmer, cover and cook until the beans are tender, 1½ hours, add more water if needed.

To prepare the sofrito:

In a separate pan heat the oil, then add the bacon, garlic, onion, pepper and stir, cook at low heat for 10 minutes, add the vinegar, tomato sauce, sherry, oregano, salt and pepper and continue cooking, stirring with wooden spoon for 15 minutes. When the beans are tender add the sofrito, stir and blend, simmer for an additional 30 minutes, the beans should be thick and rich, discard the bay leaves and serve with white or yellow rice.

MOM'S BLACK BEANS
FRIJOLES NEGROS

1 lb dried black beans, rinsed in cold water, picked over and soaked overnight in cold water to cover by 1 ½ inches, remove any beans that float to the top. (If you are in a hurry 2 cans of black beans work just fine.)
1 bay leaf
1 medium size green bell pepper, seeded and cut into quarters

For the sofrito:

¼ cup pure Spanish olive oil
3 to 4 cloves garlic, finely chopped
2 tablespoons cider vinegar (optional)
2 to 3 teaspoons ground cumin
1 large onion, finely chopped
1 medium size green bell pepper, seeded and finely chopped
1 teaspoon finely chopped seeded aji (sweet chili peppers)
1 chicken bullion cube

The next day, change the water make sure it still covers the beans by 1 ½ to 2 inches. Pour into a large saucepan, add the bay leaf and green pepper, bring to a boil over high heat, reduce the heat to low, and cook uncovered, until the beans are tender and they have almost cracked open, about 2 hours. Check the beans while they are cooking and if they need more liquid, add some hot water. Not cold!

To prepare the sofrito: In a skillet heat the oil over low heat until it is fragrant, then add the garlic, onion, and bell pepper and cook, stirring, until the onion is transparent, 8 to 10 minutes. Add the cumin, vinegar, and sweet pepper, and mix well.

Add the sofrito to the beans, mix well, and cook over low heat, covered, until the beans crack open, 30 to 40 minutes. Season to taste and serve.

If you use canned beans, add sofrito to 2 cans of beans and cook at medium heat for 20 to 30 minutes, then also add overcooked potatoes to help thicken the bean sauce. If you wish.

Serves 8

BLACK BEAN HUMMUS
"DIP" DE FRIJOLES

This dip can be made from black beans or chick peas, try it for your next party, your friends will love it and you will get lots of praise for being innovative.

1 Large can of black beans or chick peas
3 tablespoons pure Spanish olive oil
Juice of one lime
2 cloves of garlic
1 teaspoon of cumin
Salt and pepper to taste
Small amount of cilantro

Blend all the ingredients in a food processor or blender until smooth.

Cover with plastic wrap and refrigerate until ready for use. Allow the dip one hour at room temperature before serving.

PORK

ROAST SUCKLING PIG
LECHON ASADO

Christmas Eve (Noche Buena) in Aguas Buenas, Puerto Rico where I was born was a day full of major preparation. Pigs were slaughtered, skinned, seasoned and marinated overnight. The following day I would awaken to the aroma of pigs roasting in outdoor barbeque pits. The scent of roasted pork and garlic would fill the air. My family must have made great pork, for even the town mayor would order his Christmas pig from us. The Roast pork was crispy brown and the meat was so tender it would fall from the bones. That Christmas Eve and day was filled with festive music, dancing, drinking and eating. A knock on the door would follow that evening with live music as the local musicians would come by and sing (le, lo, le, lo, li) for us, and the party would start again. The musicians would be somewhat smashed from all the stops, but we always welcomed them," those nights were memorable" .

Today we can order a whole pig from our butcher. If you do, make sure you have enough room in your oven and refrigerator because your pig should marinate overnight.

You will require a large roasting pan and your pig cut in half, you can always reconstruct it after roasting.

1-10 to 15 Lb suckling pig
10 cloves of garlic
1 tablespoon of oregano
2 tablespoon of salt
2 tablespoon black peppercorns
2 cups of sour orange juice (mix of orange juice with lime or lemon juice)
2 bay leaves crumbed
1 cup Spanish olive oil for basting

The day before baking, wash the pig inside and out and allow to dry well.

In a mortar (pilon) combine the garlic, salt, peppercorns and 1 teaspoon of olive oil, beat until the mix becomes a paste. Place the pig in a large roasting pan and wash it with the orange and lime or lemon mix, then rub it inside and out with the paste, sprinkle with the bay leaves, cover the pig with aluminum foil and refrigerate overnight. This process will marinate the pig. The following day preheat the oven to 375 degrees F. remove the marinate and save for basting. Put a ball of foil in the pig's mouth to keep it open, also cover the pig's ears with foil, we don't want to burn them. Roast the pig for 1 hour then lower the temperature to 350 Degrees F. bake an additional 3 to 4 hours depending on the pig's size baste often with the oil and marinade mix and when the pig is tender uncover and remove the aluminum foil and brown for 45 minutes to 1 hour, the pig skin should be redish brown, the meat should almost fall from the bones.

At this point carefully remove the pig from the oven and place on a large service tray, surrounded with lettuce leaves, and put a apple in the pig's mouth. Serve with arroz con gandules, sweet potatoes, potato salad, tossed salad, a cold beer or a good wine, and you will be in piggy heaven for Christmas.

PORK SHOULDER
PERNIL AL HORNO

5 lbs. pork shoulder
7 garlic cloves
½ tsp black pepper
½ tsp crushed oregano
1 ½ tbsp olive oil
1 ½ tsp salt
1 small packet of Sazon Goya or ½ teaspoon of Bijol

Crush the garlic in a pilon (mortar & pestle) in a small bowl mix together the garlic, salt,

Pepper, oregano, Sazon (bijol), and olive oil, mix well.

Wash the meat and pat dry.

With a sharp knife cut the fat away from the meat keeping it all in one piece. Start at the wide end and go to the narrow end. You do not have to separate it completely, leave enough still connected so that you can flip the fat over to the side while you season the meat itself. The fat will be placed over the seasoned meat and will cook over the meat giving it more flavor. Season the side of the fat that goes over the meat with a bit of the seasoning also, just the inside. The other side, the top should only have salt.

Make very deep slits all over the meat and season the meat making sure that seasoning goes into all the slits. Put the fat back over the meat, same as it was before it was cut, and sprinkle it with salt.

Refrigerate the shoulder, covered with plastic wrap, for 24 hours.

Let the meat get back into room temperature before cooking. (Approx. 1 hour)

Place the meat in a deep pan with the fat side up. There will be a lot of grease so be sure to use a deep pan that is least 2" deep. At this point add a cup of water to the pan to avoid dryness and sticking to the pan. The fat side up will make nice crunchy pork skin.

Preheat the oven for at least 30 minutes before placing the meat inside. Cook in a 400 degree oven for one hour, and then reduce temperature to 300 degrees for about 2 hours. Cover with foil for first 2 hours, then uncover for last hour. <u>Do not turn the pork shoulder.</u>. When the pork is done, you can prick it on the side with a fork to see if it shreds. If the skin is not crispy enough for your satisfaction, then leave it in the oven and raise the temperature again to 400 degrees and cook approximately 15 minutes or so until it is crispy.

Remove the meat from the oven and let it rest on the counter for about 20-30 minutes before carving. To carve, remove the skin completely and set aside. Carve the meat and then cut the skin into pieces and place over the meat.

Masa (Vegetable dough)	*Filling*

Masa (Vegetable dough)

2 Lbs Yautia
5 Lbs Green bananas
2 Lbs Potatoes
1 Green Plantain
2 Tablespoons salt
1 ½ cup achiote (annatto) oil
1 Large bowl
2 Cans evaporated milk
1 Ball of kite string

Filling

5 to 10lb Pork shoulder Chopped into small pieces
1 chopped onion
6 garlic cloves crushed
1 green pepper chopped
8 sweet chili peppers (aji) chopped
6 sprigs of cilantro chopped
1 Large can of tomato sauce or puree
2 Large cans of chick peas (garbanzos)
1 cup red pimientos, sliced thin
1 Tablespoon salt
1 Tablespoon black pepper
1 Tablespoon oregano
1 Tablespoon adobo seasoning
1 Quart water
1 Large bowl

Pasteles have a long history, they were made for many years by Island Indians in banana leaves, In Mexico they are made out of corn meal, (Tamales), some will put ground beef as a filling, others will use stewed chicken, the masa (dough) can be made from yucca (Cassava).

Pasteles are usually made a once a year, during the month of November and you should make enough to cover Thanksgiving and Christmas. It is not a process that you should do alone, so call friends and or family members put on some music, open a bottle of wine and you will enjoy pasteles for the rest of the year.

You can start by clearing the table, have one person cut the string, you will need about 50 strands, each about 55 inches long, set them aside.

Peel about 20 to 30 green bananas using a sharp knife to make the incision into the skin, then use a butter knife to remove the skin, put the peeled bananas into a bowl with salted water, now peel the potatoes and yautia and put both into the salted water. This process will prevent them from discoloring.

Now we go on to the next step which is grating the vegetables. I prefer a hand grater; However, you can use a food processor if you have one, if not keep grating, I suggest you keep in mind that hand graters are very sharp, so stop grating when you get down to small pieces.

Some people like to do the masa (dough) the day before. I prefer to do it all on the same day. When the grating is completed add 2 tablespoons of salt, one tablespoon of pepper,

169

2 cans of evaporated milk and ½ cup of colored oil (achiote) blend well with a large spoon, your masa is complete, refrigerator until you are ready to make the pasteles.

Making the filling (pork shoulder

Take a large 5 to 10 Lb. pork shoulder remove the outer pork skin and de-bone it, cut the pork meat into 1 ½ inch pieces. Put the cut meat into a large kettle with 1 quart of water, boil for ½ hour then add the peppers, onions, garbanzos, garlic, cilantro, tomato sauce, salt and pepper, and the adobo seasoning, cook at medium heat for and additional 1/2 hour stirring constantly. Remove from heat and allow to cool. Do not overcook the meat filling; keep in mind that the pasteles will require boiling later on for 1 hour. That process will complete the cooking of the meat and the masa.

Ok. lets move on. You will need about 50 pieces of parchment paper, you can also use Banana leaves or both, but the parchment paper by itself works just fine.

Now for the Assembly line

In bowl #1 have the masa (filling).
In bowl #2 the pork stuffing in sauce.
Parchment paper
1 cup Achiote oil
Large spoon for masa
Large spoon for filling
Teaspoon for oil

On a parchment paper, put a teaspoon of oil in the center and spread to cover area where the masa will be placed. *see illustration. Next put a heaping serving spoon full of masa on the oily area on the parchment paper center. Make a well in the center of the masa by pressing down on the center in a circular motion. Next add about 5 pieces of the filling with it's juices into the well in the center of the masa. The rest is folding and tying.

Tie the pastel. Simply make sure the folds are pressed securely. Tie the pastel with string to hold it together. Make one run of string lengthwise and two runs the other way. This will hold the parchment paper secure. *See illustration.

The final part is Boiling water in a large kettle (pot) with 2 tablespoons of salt. Once the water is boiling then lower the pasteles in and boil uncovered for 1 hour, cut string and the pastels should slide from the paper to the plate.

CABBAGE PASTELES

1 Cabbage, weighing about 3 lbs
4 Quarts water
2 tablespoons salt

To make leaves pliable, place cabbage, stem down, in water with salt, cover, and boil at moderate heat for 20 minutes.

Drain, and reserve the water to boil the pasteles. Thrust a knife through center of cabbage, and remove leaves, one at a time.

Turn cabbage leaves over and carefully press down central ridge of each leaf to level it, without breaking the leaf

The leaf process is done by putting a leaf on the parchment paper that has been oiled; the leaf will now hold the masa and the filing. Think of stuffed cabbage.

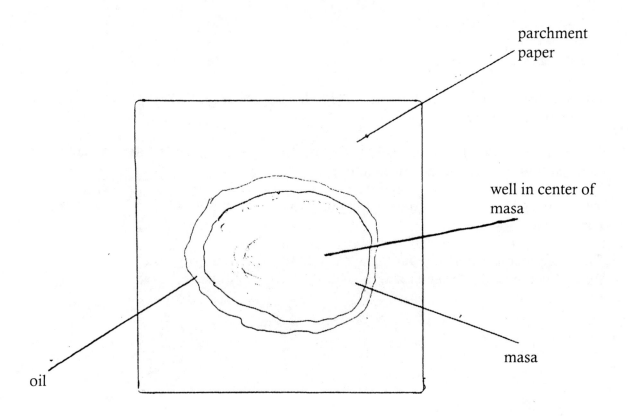

parchment
paper

well in center of
masa

masa

oil

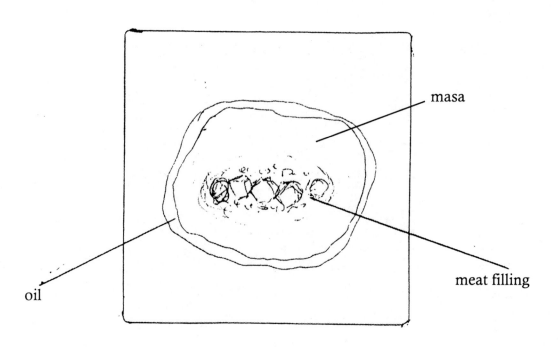

masa

oil

meat filling

1.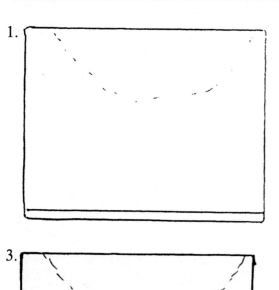

2.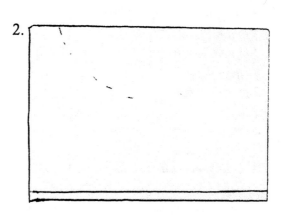

3.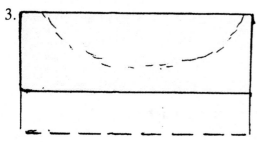

4.

6.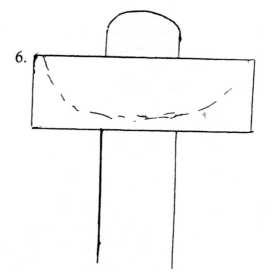

5.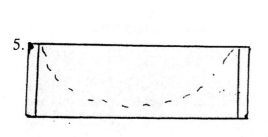

7.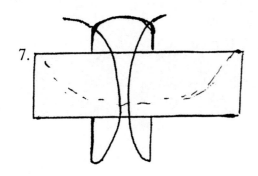

8.

PASTELES DE YUCCA

4 cups grated yucca
1 lb fresh pork
1 ounce fresh bacon
1 sweet pepper
1 green pepper
1 tomato
1 leaf coriander (culantro)
1 teaspoon salt
4 tablespoons Annatto oil (achiote)
¼ cup milk
¼ cup olives
1 onion
4 tablespoons corn or vegetable oil
2 tablespoons capers
2 ounces ham
Banana leaves – 1 per pastel

Shred the Yucca and squeeze through Cheesecloth to get the starch out.

Mix the oil, salt, and milk, mixing well, to the texture of pancakes.

Cut the ham, bacon, and pork meat into very small pieces.

In a large saucepan, cook all the meat in the oil with salt, tomato, coriander, (cilantro) peppers and onion until the meat is tender. Seasoning to taste.

After everything is cooked, add the olives and capers.

Cut the Banana leaves into approximately 10 x 10" squares and wilt them over low heat on the stove.

Wet the center of the leaf with annatto oil (achiote) and place about 5 or 6 tablespoons of the yucca mix in the center. Using a spoon, form a well in the center of the mixture and place about 2 tablespoons of the meat mixture in the well. Carefully fold the leaf over, in order to cover the meat with yucca on all sides. Do not over stuff them. Tie them with cooking twine.

Repeat this procedure until all the yucca mixture has been used.

Boil the wrapped pasteles on high heat for an hour and serve.

TRIPE A LA CRIOLLA
MONDONGO

4-1/2 Lbs beef tripe, trimmed
1 lb pigs feet
2-1/2 quarts water

2 green peppers, seeded and chopped
4 cloves garlic, peeled and chopped
6 fresh cilantro leaves and chopped
8 sweet chili peppers chopped
2 medium onions chopped
2 tablespoons salt
2 ears of corn cut into pieces
2 carrots cut small
1 cans garbanzos (chick peas)
2 potatoes cut small
1 lb yautia peeled and cut into 1-1/2 inch pieces
1 lb pumpkin peeled and cut into 1–½ inch pieces
1 teaspoon bijol
1 teaspoon black pepper

Wash tripe and pigs feet thoroughly under running water. Put into large kettle or pot, boil for ½ hour drain water and repeat the process three times until tripe and pig's feet are tender.

Remove tripe from water, allow to cool then cut tripe into 1-1/2 inch pieces and place back in large kettle together with pig's feet and add all the above vegetables with enough water to cover all the ingredients including garbanzos with liquid. Season with salt, pepper, garlic and bijol. Boil for 30 to 45 minutes or until vegetables are cooked and the broth thickens. Allow to cool 10/15 minutes.

Serve with rice as side dish

Serves 10 to 12

GANDINGA

4 Lbs hog's gandinga (liver, kidney, and heart)
1 quart water
2 ounces lean and cured ham, washed and diced
1 onion, peeled
½ teaspoon whole dried oregano
1 green pepper, seeded and chopped
1 teaspoon bijol
2 sweet chili peppers, seeded and chopped
1 clove garlic, peeled and chopped
4 fresh cilantro leaves, chopped
2 tablespoons olive oil
½ cup tomato sauce
1 lb potatoes, peeled and cubed
1 tablespoon capers
1 tablespoon vinegar
3-1/2 teaspoons salt
10 pimiento olives

Step 1. In a large pot or kettle put in the gandinga (liver, heart, and kidneys) boil for 15 minutes. Take out the gandinga, place aside and allow to cool, reserve the water

Cut the gandinga into small 2 inch pieces and put back into the water.

Step 2. In a pre-heated deep frying pan add 2 tablespoons olive oil followed by the ham, brown the ham, stirring for 5 minutes, reduce heat to low and add the onion, green peppers, sweet chili peppers, garlic, cilantro, oregano, and bijol. Sauté for 10 minutes stirring constantly. Then add all the ingredients to large pot with the gandinga, cover and simmer for about 2 hours.

Uncover, and cook until sauce thickens

Serve with white rice.

Serves 6 to 8

BEEF

PUERTO RICAN BEEF STEW
CARNE GUISADA PUERTORIQUEÑA

1 tablespoon vegetable or corn oil
2 lbs trimmed beef top round, cut into 3 inch chunks, and floured
1 green pepper, seeded, and chopped
2 onions, peeled and chopped
4 cloves garlic, peeled and chopped
6 fresh culantro leaves, washed and chopped
½ teaspoon whole dried oregano, crushed
1 quart water
½ cup tomato sauce
2 bay leaves
1 teaspoon salt
4 carrots, scraped, and cut into ½ inch rounds
1 can (1lb 1 ounce) green peas
½ lb potatoes, peeled, and quartered
8 pimiento stuffed olives
1 tablespoon capers

In a large pre-heated Caldero or heavy kettle, heat the vegetable or corn oil. Add the chunks of beef and stir constantly over moderate-high heat until browned.

Add water, green pepper, onions, garlic, culantro, oregano, tomato sauce, bay leaves, and 1 tablespoon salt. Mix and bring to a boil. Reduce heat to low, cover, and cook for

1½ hour.

Add the carrots potatoes and continue cooking for ½ hour , then add the olives, capers, and peas to the mix, stir, lower the heat to a simmer and cook at low heat for 10 to 15 more minutes while sauce thickens. Allow to cool and serve with rice on the side.

OX TAIL STEW
RABO GUISADO

5 lbs ox tails
1 green pepper, chopped fine
1 onion, chopped fine
4 garlic cloves crushed
1 large can of tomatoes or tomato puree
1 beef bullion cube
½ teaspoon oregano
½ teaspoon cumin
½ teaspoon ground black pepper
1 teaspoon salt
juice of one lime
2 chorizos (Spanish sausage) sliced into 1 inch pieces
4 potatoes peeled and quartered
½ cup dry red wine
½ cup white wine or dry sherry
¼ cup olive oil
2 cups of water
large kettle or pot

In a bowl put in the oxtail, sprinkle with salt, pepper and lime juice,

In a large kettle over medium heat add ¼ cup olive oil, and the oxtails and brown on all sides, transfer the ox tail back to the bowl. In the same kettle now add the onion, pepper and garlic, stirring for about 6 minutes. Return the oxtail to the kettle and add all the ingredients, except the potatoes, stir well and bring to a boil over medium heat, reduce the heat to low, cover, and simmer for 1 1/2 hours, add additional water if needed, then add the potatoes and cook an additional 30 minutes until the potatoes are done.

Serve with white rice.

**Hint: If you want your oxtail stew done in a rich brown gravy, omit the tomatoes or tomato sauce puree, and add 2 tablespoons of soy sauce, and 2 tablespoons of teriyaki sauce. Your sauce will now take on a brown gravy color, rich and delicious.

In addition the same recipe (above) applies to;

Stewed short ribs
Regular ribs
Beef stew
Pork chops
Steaks

They can all become stewed in this manner and, Remember which style of sauce you want.

If red, add red wine and tomato sauce or puree

For dark gravy add dry wine, soy sauce and teriyaki sauce

SPANISH BEEF HASH
PICADILLO

¼ cup pure Spanish olive oil
1 medium size onion, chopped
1 medium size green bell pepper, seeded and chopped
2 to 3 cloves garlic, finely chopped
1 lb ground beef, chuck or rump
¼ cup dry sherry
½ cup canned crushed tomatoes or prepared tomato sauce

For the garnish

1 large egg, hard boiled and finely chopped
1 tablespoon Worcestershire sauce, optional
1 small all purpose potato, peeled and cut into ¼ inch cubes
¼ cup dark raisins
½ cup pimiento stuffed green olives (may be cut in halves), drained.
¼ cup vegetable or peanut oil
½ cup drained canned early sweet peas
1 pimiento, chopped

In a casserole, heat the oil over low heat until fragrant, then add the onion, bell pepper, and garlic, and cook stirring, 10 minutes. Add the beef and cook, stirring, until brown, 10 to 15 minutes, breaking up any large chunks with a wooden spoon. Drain off any excess fat.

Add the sherry, tomatoes, salt, worcestershire and tabasco, stir, and cook, uncovered, over medium heat for 15 to 20 minutes.

Heat the vegetable oil in a small skillet over medium high heat until fragrant, then fry the chopped potato until golden, 10 minutes.(if you prefer not to fry the potato, boil it over medium high heat, peeled and cubed, in salted water to cover until tender 20 minutes, and omit the vegetable oil.) Add the potato, raisins, and olives to the meat, correct the seasonings, and continue cooking until most of the liquid is absorbed, 10 to 15 minutes.

Transfer the picadillo to a large bowl or platter, place the chopped egg in the center, outline the border with peas, and sprinkle the entire dish with the pimiento.

OLD CLOTHES
ROPA VIEJA

1-2 ½ lb flank steak, cut in half
2 bay leaves
¼ cup pure spanish olive oil
1 large onion cut in half and each half thinly sliced
1 large green bell pepper, seeded and cut into thin strips
2 to 3 cloves garlic, finely chopped
2 cups drained and chopped canned whole tomatoes
½ teaspoon salt
½ teaspoon pepper
½ cup finely chopped drained pimientos for garnish
½ cup cooking sherry

Place the beef and 1 bay leaf in a large saucepan, cover with salted water, and cook over low heat, covered, until the meat is tender, 1 to 1 ½ hours. Remove the meat from the stock (save the stock), allow the meat to cool at room temperature, then cut the meat into 2 inch chunks.

Meanwhile, in a large skillet, heat the oil over low heat until fragrant, then cook the onions, bell pepper, and garlic, stirring, or until the onions are tender, 6 to 8 minutes. Add the tomatoes, sherry, and the remaining stock, bay leaf, and cook, uncovered, an additional 15 minutes.

When the meat is cool, shred it with your fingers, season with salt and pepper, add it to the tomato mixture, cover, and simmer over low heat for 30 minutes. Remove the bay leaves, garnish with the pimientos and peas, and serve with white rice (arroz blanco).

The dish can be prepared a day or two in advance, cooled, and refrigerated, and then simmered, covered, over low heat until heated for 10 to 15 minutes.

LIVER, BACON AND ONIONS
HIGADO CON SEBOLLA Y TOSINETTA

"Liver and onions", yes liver and onions. Liver is a very nutritious and still an inexpensive meal, and if liver is done right you should be able to cut it with a spoon, it should never be as hard as the sole of a shoe. I guarantee that if you follow my recipe you will have an enjoyable and delicious meal, and you will probably eat liver more often.

3 to 4 pieces of liver, cow or calf, the calf's liver is tenderer, but both are fine for this dish.
3 Cloves of garlic, crushed
¼ cup of olive oil
2 medium onions, sliced
6 to 8 slices of bacon
¼ teaspoon salt
¼ teaspoon black pepper
¼ teaspoon oregano
2 Eggs
½ cup flour
½ cup white sherry or any white wine
1 stick of butter
1 lemon or lime

The night before, wash liver, pat dry and put into a plastic container, prick the liver with a fork on both sides, add the juice of a lemon, and half of the olive oil, season with salt, pepper, oregano and add the crushed garlic, turn several times, then cover and refrigerate overnight. This process will give you a liver that has the flavor of garlic, oregano and olive oil.

The following day scramble the eggs and add the liver then transfer the liver into a plate of flour, turn several times coating all sides. Now heat a frying pan at medium heat add the remaining olive oil and a stick of butter, put in the liver and fry for 5 minutes on both sides, lower the heat, add the wine and the sliced onions, cover pan and continue cooking until onions are soft, about 10 minutes. On a side pan fry the bacon, and put on top of the liver and onions. Serve with mashed potatoes and buttered corn.

Serves 4

SMOTHERED KID (GOAT)
CABRO ESTOFADO

5 lbs tender kid (goat) meat, trimmed
½ cup lemon juice

Seasoning

4 cloves garlic, peeled	*Crush and mix in a mortar*
1 tablespoon whole dried oregano	"
½ teaspoon ground pepper	"
2 tablespoons salt	"
1 tablespoon vinegar	"
1 tablespoon olive oil	"

12 stuffed pimento olives
2 tablespoons capers
1 lb onions, peeled and sliced
3 bay leaves
2 cups water

2 cups dry wine
1/3 cup sugar
1 ½ pounds potatoes, peeled and cut in pieces

Wash meat and cut into 2-inch chunks. Soak in lemon juice and set in refrigerator for several hours or overnight. Drain and rinse rapidly in cool water

Place kid (goat) meat in a large caldero or heavy kettle and rub with Seasoning outlined above.

Add the olives, capers, onions, bay leaves, and 2 cups water. Bring rapidly to a boil, cover, and boil over moderate heat for 2 hours.

Add the wine, sugar, and potatoes, cover, and boil over moderate heat about 45 minutes, or until meat is tender.

Uncover, and boil over moderate heat until sauce thickens to taste.

Serve with rice

Serves 12

Dolores (doll) supports many causes throughout New York and we 're always invited to Attend many catered functions. Dolores always invites her friends and we dress up in our Sunday best for a wonderful night of music, dancing, drinking and eating, eating, and more eating. Someone please tell these establishments that people don't require that much food to have a good time. No wonder people in this country are obese, o.k. I'm not just blaming the catering halls, but let us see what happens. We enter the hall, greet our many friends and proceed to find our seats. Next we get drinks and on to the food area. We get a plate and get on line for the appetizers which includes roast pork, turkey, beef, chicken, meatballs, sausages with onions and peppers, eggplant, various seafood, paella, pastas, salads, cheeses, fruits, and the kitchen sink. The funny part is that some of the invited guest, myself included, think that the appetizers are the main course and we fill up two plates with every item. We stuff our faces, go for another drink and the appetizer area is clear and its time to dance and enjoy the evening music, (belly full) good to go. Our table has many beautiful smiling faces of our friends and Sara's asking me to dance, when a waiter appears and puts a plate of decorated fruit in front of me. I don't think about it much as I eat the fruit and proceed to the dance floor. Minutes later Sara and I return to our seats to find a salad waiting for us. I eat part of the salad and get up to dance with Dolores and no sooner do we get back, there's a bowl of vodka penne waiting for us. By now I'm starting to think" This must be my last meal or did I die and went to food heaven ". I eat a little of the penne, since I don't want to waste food, and another though occurs to me. If I don't get up to go dance, maybe it will stop. " Fat chance " Here comes the waiter again, and this time he wants to know what I want as a main course, " HA " and he has choices, Steak, Chicken or Seafood he says. I selected the Steak. Dolores orders the chicken, so we can share, she says, like I want to share more food. Another beer and a few more dances and the waiter arrives with the main course. Steak with potato and string beans. I 'm looking at the plate wondering, where am I going to put this; and Is this madness ever going to end. I do my best to eat but most of the food ends up in a doggie bag to go. Thank goodness the music is kicking and we 're able to dance some of the food off; Is it over? " No "for here he comes again, this time he has cake and coffee. Kidding around I say to the waiter, Yo waiter more food. He gives me this strange look; I'm sure glad he didn't take me seriously.

Having a good time with the girls at a fund raiser
Alicia, Dolores, her sister Teresa, Sara and Liz

Doll and Julio

Doll and Mitzy

ITALIAN

LASAGNA

Hispanics in general love Italian food. Doll and I visit Rino's Ristorante in the Bronx every Tuesday for delicious Northern Italian cuisine, and we are always greeted by a friendly hug, kisses and a smile from Gaspar, Rino's co owner and chef. Rino's has become a favorite Italian restaurant for many of their special dishes, one of which is Lasagna. Lasagna can be made so many different ways but the most popular still is the meat lasagna (ground beef) yet today many meat sauces are also made with ground pork and ground veal.

1 Lb ground beef
1 lb ground pork and ground veal
2 cans 35 oz Italian plum tomatoes
¼ cup virgin olive oil
1 large onion chopped
1 garlic clove crushed
1 teaspoon salt
4 bay leaves
1½ teaspoon oregano
6 to 8 fresh basil leaves
1 large 4 to 5 quart pot
1 cup dry white wine
1/3 cup tomato paste
3 to 4 cups of water

Heat pot over medium heat, add the olive oil then the onions and cook, stirring occasionally, until the onion are golden, about 7 minutes, add the garlic and ground beef, pork and veal , cook uncovered turning until the meat becomes pale; season with salt and continue cooking until the meat starts to turn brown, about 5 minutes stir and break up the meat; add bay leaves and oregano, Pour in the tomatoes and tomato paste, stir until paste is dissolved, Bring to a boil, then lower the heat to a simmer and cook uncovered, stirring often until the sauce becomes deep red in color about 1 1/2 hours, add the wine and water (hot) slowly stirring and cook an additional ½ hour. Skim excess oil from top. This recipe will give you perfectly seasoned thick sauce for you lasagna. Now for the noodles.

Noodles for lasagna, serves 12

2 Lbs of lasagna noodles or 1 large packed box
2 tablespoons of olive oil
2 lbs of packaged whole milk ricotta cheese
2 large eggs
2 cups of Parmigiano cheese
1 lb mozzarella cheese, sliced thin (prefer fresh)
1 tablespoon of salt

In a large pot boil water at medium heat, add the salt and olive oil, this will help to stop the noodles from sticking together, carefully add the noodles to the hot water and cook uncovered, moving the noodles as they cook ,do not over cook remember they will also cook in the oven. Cook noodles "al dente" or half cooked 5 minutes should do it. Turn off the heat and remove the noodles quickly into a large bowl of cold iced water, this process will stop the noodles from being overdone. Next beat the eggs and add the ricotta cheese, stir until well blended. Preheat your oven to 375 degrees F.

To assemble the lasagna, spoon about a cup of the sauce on the bottom of a large baking pan, arrange the noodles lengthwise as to cover the bottom. Cover the noodles with 1 or 2 cups of sauce, sprinkle in about ½ cup of the grated cheese, arrange the noodles crosswise over the cheese, and cut the overhanging noodles. Next spread the ricotta mixture evenly over the noodles, arrange more noodles lengthwise over the ricotta. Arrange the sliced mozzarella in an even layer over the noodles, cover again with sauce, and sprinkle ½ cup of grated cheese with sauce. Repeat the process until complete. Cover with aluminum foil and bake for 45 minutes, remove the cover and continue baking for an additional 20 minutes until the top is crusty around the edges, take out and allow it to rest for 30 minutes before cutting and serving. Lasagna takes a lot of work but it's worth every minute, and leftovers freeze well, and will taste better the next day.

Lasagna Variables; Eggplant, Use sliced and floured eggplant for the noodles after frying slices in oil.

Vegetable Lasagnas, tomatoe , roasted peppers, cabbage, zuccuni,, mushrooms, spinach, onions, carrots, and many other vegetables can be used in making lasagna.

Doll's son Derek (Mr. Boriqua Fitness) Batista, scarfing up some lasagne

MEATBALLS
ALBONDIGAS

2 lbs ground beef
1 small onion, minced
1 small green pepper, minced
1 egg
½ teaspoon of salt
½ teaspoon of pepper
1 garlic clove, crushed
½ teaspoon oregano
½ teaspoon ground or fresh basil
1 cup bread crumbs
1 large can Italian tomatoes
1 large can of tomato sauce or puree
1 quart of water
½ cup red dry wine
1 mixing bowl

Blend The beef, onion, egg, salt, pepper, garlic, oregano, basil, bread crumbs, together in a bowl, then make or shape the meatballs, small, medium, or large. (I like large meatballs)

After the meatballs are done, in a large sauce pan heat water then add the tomatoes, puree, onion, pepper, and seasonings, simmer uncovered for ½ hour, stirring constantly.

Now add your meatballs and the wine and continue simmering for an additional ½ hour.

Skim of any fat that surfaces. Serves 8

Meatballs are great because once you prepare them you can complete the cooking process in various ways. The recipe above is for making meatballs Italian style. If you are going to put the meatballs into a sauce make sure that the sauce is hot, this will allow the finished product to be firm and juicy. The egg is a binder that helps to hold the meatball together. Meatballs can be put into a pre heated oven and baked at 350 degrees for 30 to 40 minutes, make sure that the pan contains a small amount of wine or water to insure that the meatballs do not stick to the bottom of the pan.

*You can make Swedish meatballs by putting them into a cream sauce (béchamel sauce) or you can add spices like curry powder to the mix and have curried meatballs.

*Hint if in a hurry you can open up a jar of good Italian sauce, heat, drop in the meatballs and simmer for 30 minutes, serve over boiled spaghetti or white rice. Or you can put them in a hero sandwich for lunch. Meatballs make a great party appetizer, or if you like make a giant meatball which we call meatloaf with mashed potatoes and fresh buttered corn. MMMM Comfort food.

MARINARA SAUCE
SALSA MARINARA

¼ cup extra virgin olive oil
8 cloves garlic, peeled
3 lbs ripe fresh plum tomatoes peeled and seeded or one 35 ounce can peeled plum tomatoes,
seeded and lightly crushed with their liquid.
Dash of Salt (optional)
Dash of Crushed hot red pepper (optional)
10 fresh basil leaves, torn into small pieces.

Heat the oil in a 2 to 3 quart nonreactive saucepan over medium heat

Whack the garlic with the flat side of a knife, add it to the oil, and cook until lightly browned about 2 minutes.

Carefully slide the tomatoes and their liquid into the oil. Bring to a boil and season lightly with salt and crushed red pepper. Lower the heat so the sauce is at a lively simmer and cook, breaking up the tomatoes with a whisk or spoon, until the sauce is chunky and thick, about 20 minutes. Stir in the basil about 5 minutes before the sauce is finished. Taste the sauce and season with salt and red pepper if necessary.

Makes enough to cover 6 servings of pasta.

Dolores (Doll) and family at Rino's once a year reunion celebration

GARLIC BREAD

1 loaf Italian bread
2 teaspoons finely chopped garlic
2 tablespoons finely chopped fresh flat leaf parsley
pinch of pepper
pinch of salt
½ stick (1/4 cup) unsalted butter, softened
1 tablespoon extra virgin olive oil
1 tomato cut in half
½ cup parmesan cheese
Preheat over to 350 degrees F.

Mince and mash garlic to a paste using a mortar and pestle or (pilon). Stir together butter, oil, and garlic paste in a bowl until smooth, then stir in parsley.

Cut the bread length wise in half , rub the tomato on the bread, spread the garlic butter on the bread now add the parmesan cheese.

Wrap loaf in foil and bake in middle of oven 15 minutes. Open foil and bake 5 minutes more.

Serves 4 to 6

Doll's parade of beauties (Our friends) at a Bar B Que at sister Teresa's house

Cousin Yvonne and Dolores in London

TO CLEAN AND STEAM MUSSELS

1 ¼ TO 4 ½ lb cultivated mussels
1 cup liquid; you may use water, or a mix of water and white wine or beer.

Scrub each mussel shell with a brush under cold water, scraping off any barnacles with a knife. If byssus (beard) is still attached, remove it just before cooking by pulling it from tip to hinge or cutting it off with a knife. Bring liquid to a boil in a 4 to 6 quart heavy pot, then reduce heat to moderate and cook mussels, covered, stirring occasionally, until mussels are opened, 3 to 6 minutes, checking frequently after 3 minutes and transferring as opened to a bowl, (discard any unopened mussels after 6 minutes.)

PASTA WITH MUSSELS AND CHORIZO

4 Lb. mussels, cleaned and steamed, then shucked
2 Spanish chorizo links (spicy cured pork sausage: ½ lb total).
½ cup white wine
½ cup extra virgin olive oil
2 shallots, finely chopped
1 tablespoon minced garlic
1 lb dried pasta
2 tablespoons fresh lemon juice
¼ cup finely chopped fresh flat leaf parsley
½ cup finely chopped fresh cilantro

Heat oil in a 12 inch heavy skillet over moderately high heat until hot but not smoking, then sauté chorizo and shallots, stirring until chorizo is golden brown on edges, about 4 minutes. Add garlic and sauté, stirring, 1 minute, add wine and simmer until liquid is reduced by half, about 5 minutes. Keep sauce warm, covered.

Cook pasta in a large pot of boiling salted water until al dente, then reserve 1 cup pasta cooking water and drain pasta in a colander. Return pasta to pot and add sauce, mussels, parsley, cilantro and ½ cup pasta cooking water. Cook over low heat, stirring until mussels are heated through. Add more cooking water if pasta seems dry.

Toss pasta with lemon juice and salt and pepper to taste

Serves 6 to 8

MUSHROOMS

Mushrooms are a wonderful and easy to prepare vegetable. They can be sautéed or stuffed with almost anything you can whip up, they can be a side dish or the main course, and it's all up to you. The most popular mushroom on the market is the white button mushroom; however you will see brown button mushrooms and Portobello's, plus other varieties in your supermarket to choose from.

If you decide to wash the mushrooms do so at cooking time, don't allow the mushrooms to soak in water for long, they absorb water. Mushrooms are for the most part clean and simply require a wiping or brushing.

Remember that when stuffing a mushroom you can remove the stem, chop it up and mix it in with other items to fill the mushroom.

SAUTEED GARLIC MUSHROOMS

1 Lb button mushrooms (white or brown)
6 Tablespoons of olive oil
3 Garlic cloves, crushed
salt and pepper to taste
2 Tablespoons of chopped parsley

Wipe the mushrooms clean, and then trim the stem near to the mushroom cap, leaving part of the stem on the mushroom. You can save the stems and use them in a soup or stock. Heat a fry pan or skillet at medium high heat then add the olive oil and then the garlic, followed by the mushrooms, sauté the mushrooms stirring constantly until brown, lower the heat to low for a minute this will allow the juices in the mushroom to come out, then increase the heat to high and continue stirring until the juices have evaporated then drizzle the lemon or lime juice and stir in the parsley, turn off the heat and stir again and serve.

It's a great appetizer or side dish, Serves 4 to 6.

STUFFED MUSHROOMS WITH BREAD AND BACON

24 Button mushrooms, wiped clean and stems removed, chop the stems and use for stuffing.

Stuffing
Mushrooms stems, chopped fine
½ onion, chopped fine
½ green pepper, chopped fine
½ celery stalk, chopped fine
1 garlic clove, crushed fine
2 sprigs of parsley, chopped fine
6 slices of bread cut into cubes
1 cup of chicken stock
½ stick of butter
8 bacon strips fried and chopped fine
4 tablespoons olive oil

In a heated frying pan, add the olive oil, butter, celery, onion, pepper, garlic and stir for 3 minutes, add the chopped mushroom stems, and continue sautéing and stirring for 3 more minutes, then add the bread, chicken stock and blend well, now add the bacon and parsley, mix well and you are ready to stuff mushrooms. Use a teaspoon and fill mushroom. See illustration. Set in baking pan lined with aluminum foil bake uncovered for 30 minutes and party on.

stuffing

mushroom cap

DESSERTS

CLASSIC YELLOW CAKE
BIZCOCHO CLASICO

12 tablespoons (1-1/2 sticks, 6 ounces) butter
1-3/4 cups (12 ½ ounces sugar)
¾ teaspoon salt
2 ½ teaspoons baking powder
2 teaspoons vanilla extract

4 large eggs, plus 2 yolks
2 ¾ cups (1-1/2 ounces) unbleached all purpose flour
1- ½ cups milk

Preheat the oven to 350 degrees F.

In a large mixing bowl, Blend the cream and butter, sugar, salt, baking powder, and vanilla until fluffy and light, at least 5 minutes.

Add the eggs to the butter mixture one at a time, beating well after each addition. Slowly blend one third of the flour into the creamed mixture, then half the milk, another third of the flour, the remaining milk, and the remaining flour. Be sure to scrape the sides and bottom of the bowl occasionally throughout this process.

Pour the batter into greased and floured or parchment lined 8 or 9 inch round pan or a 9 x 13-inch pan. Bake for 23 to 26 minutes (for 8 inch pans), 25 to 30 minutes (for 9 inch pans), or about 35 minutes for the 9 x 13 inch pan. Remove the cakes from the oven, cool for10 minutes in the pan, then turn out on a rack to cool completely before frosting.

*This cake is perfect if you wish to make Strawberry short cake. Just cut a square of the yellow cake add strawberries and top with fresh whipped cream.

CHOCOLATE CAKE

Hmmm Chocolate devils food cake, this cake has an appropriate name "Devil", because it is so sinfully delicious. This cake is moist, deep dark and you can decorate it with a number of frosting; chocolate, white, peanut butter, or coconut frosting to name a few.

5 large eggs
1 ½ cups of milk or water
2 cups unbleached all purpose flour
2 teaspoons vanilla extract
1 ½ to 2 sticks of butter
1 ½ to 2 cups of superfine or granulated sugar
½ teaspoon salt
1 ½ teaspoons baking soda
¾ to one cup of natural cocoa powder

Preheat oven to 350° F

In a large mixing bowl, (metal or plastic) blend the sugar, butter, salt and vanilla until light and fluffy about 5 minutes. In a separate bowl whisk together cocoa and flour, I would sift the four, (less lumps), add the eggs to the butter mix, one at a time and continue beating the mix with each egg, now slowly blend the flour mix into the creamed mixture along with the milk or water, make sure all the ingredients are mixed well, no lumps. Butter and flour two 9 inch round cake pans, divide the batter evenly between the pans, bake the cakes for 30 to 35 minutes, test by sticking a toothpick into the center, it should come out clean. Remove the cakes from the oven, cool for 8 to 10 minutes then remove from the pan, now it is time to decide on what to use for a filling, this part I leave to you, it can be frosting, jelly, pudding, fruits, yogurt, or a mix of any two items.

RICE PUDDING
ARROZ CON DULCE

In making rice pudding simply remember that what your producing is sweetened over cooked rice with raisins. It's a perfect holiday type dessert.

1 cup of rice (white)
4 cups of water
1 small box of raisins
1 can of condensed milk
1 can evaporated milk
1 cup regular milk
½ cup sugar
1 teaspoon vanilla extract
½ teaspoon cinnamon
½ teaspoon ground cloves
½ teaspoon ground nutmeg

Start by heating a 2 quart sauce pan filled with 4 cups of water. Once the water is hot put in the rice and stir. Reduce the heat to medium. Cook the rice until the water is absorbed, about 10 to15 minutes Stir the rice, than cover the pot, lower the heat to low and continue cooking for another 10 minutes, Stir once more than add all the remaining ingredients and again continue cooking at low heat while stirring for 5 more minutes. We Hispanics like then put the mixture on a large platter and allow it to cool until cold. Then we sprinkle cinnamon on top and serve it in slices, like a pie. you can put the rice mix in separate wine glasses and serve with whipped cream and a cherry on top." Yummy"

Serves 6 to 8 portions

TRADITIONAL FLAN

1 cup sugar
2 cups milk
Pinch of salt

1 large egg
6 large egg yolks
1 teaspoon vanilla extract

1 cinnamon stick or ½ teaspoon ground cinnamon

In a small, heavy saucepan over medium heat, cook ½ cup of the sugar, stirring after it starts to bubble, until it caramelizes, 6 to 8 minutes. Pour it into a 2-quart ovenproof mold, swirl to coat the bottom, and set aside. Preheat the oven to 350 degrees F.

In a heavy saucepan over low heat, simmer the milk, salt, the remaining sugar, and the cinnamon until the sugar dissolves. Remove from heat and let cool to room temperature.

In a bowl mix the whole egg and egg yolks. Slowly pour the egg mixture into the cooled milk, stir, add the vanilla, and mix well.

Pour the mixture into the caramelized pan, set it into a larger pan on the middle oven rack, and pour lukewarm water into the outer pan, reaching two thirds of the way up the side of the custard.

Bake 1 hour, uncover, and insert a cake tester in the center to see if it is set, if the custard is wobbly, it is not done. If not set, cook the custard, uncovered another 15 minutes. Remove from the oven and the water bath, let cool to room temperature, cover, and refrigerate 2 to 3 hours.

To serve, run a knife around the inside edges of the pan, invert the custard onto a serving plate, and spoon the caramel or whipped cream over the custard.

COCONUT CUSTARD
FLAN DE COCO

1 cup sugar
2 cups half and half or light cream
4 large eggs, lightly beaten
2 large egg yolks

½ cup tightly packed finely chopped shredded sweetened coconut
½ teaspoon vanilla extract
fresh berries for garnish

Preheat the oven to 350 degrees F. In a small, heavy saucepan over medium heat, cook ½ cup of he sugar, stirring constantly after it starts to bubble, until it caramelizes, 6 to 8 minutes. Divide the syrup among 8 custard cups, and set aside

In a medium size heavy saucepan over medium heat, heat the half and half and sugar almost to scalding, and set aside.

In a large bowl, whisk the eggs and yolks together until blended. Gradually add the cooled half and half, coconut, and vanilla, and mix well.

Pour the mixture into the prepared custard cups, place in a large pan, and fill the outer pan with lukewarm water two thirds the height of the cups or mold. Bake 1 hour for a large mold and slightly less for custard cups, or until a cake tester inserted in the flan comes out clean. Remove from the water, allow to cool to room temperature, cover, and refrigerate.

To unmold, run a knife along the inner edge of the mold or cups and invert the custard onto a plate. Spoon the caramel over the top and garnish with fresh berries or whipped cream.

BREAD PUDDING
PUDIN DE PAN

In Doll's kitchen we do a lot of dinner entertaining and many times people bring breads of all types. Much of that bread ends up in the freezer, so every three months I end up making bread pudding.

1 or 2 loaves of stale bread
4 to 6 eggs
½ teaspoon vanilla extract
½ teaspoon cinnamon powder or 6 cinnamon sticks
1 stick of butter (melted)
½ teaspoon nutmeg
½ teaspoon apple spice (optional)
1 cup of sugar
2 cups of milk
1 small can of sweetened condensed milk
1 can evaporated milk
1 small box of raisins

Soak your bread in water to soften, break into small pieces, drain and squeeze out most of the water. In a separate bowl beat eggs and blend in all the other ingredients, combine with the bread and pour mix into a baking pan. Preheat oven to 350 degrees F. Bake uncovered for 1 hour, lower heat to 300 degrees F. and continue baking for an additional 30 minutes until golden brown. Take out and allow to cool and set. Serve with whipped cream, and don't forget the neighbors.

CPSIA information can be obtained
at www.ICGtesting.com
Printed in the USA
FFOW01n2145071117
43403817-42008FF